Augustine and the Pelagian Controversy

The Doctrines and Theology of Pelagius in the Early Christian Church

By Benjamin B. Warfield

Published by Pantianos Classics

ISBN-13: 978-1-78987-015-2

First published in 1897

Contents

Part One – The Origin & Nature of Pelgagianism 4

Part Two - The External History of the Pelagian Controversy 12

Part Three - Augustine's Part in The Controversy 20

Part Four - The Theology of Grace 95

Part One – The Origin & Nature of Pelagianism

It was inevitable that the energy of the Church in intellectually realizing and defining its doctrines in relation to one another, should first be directed towards the objective side of Christian truth. The chief controversies of the first four centuries and the resulting definitions of doctrine, concerned the nature of God and the person of Christ; and it was not until these theological and Christological questions were well upon their way to final settlement, that the Church could turn its attention to the more subjective side of truth. Meanwhile she bore in her bosom a full recognition, side by side, of the freedom of the will, the evil consequences of the fall, and the necessity of divine grace for salvation. Individual writers, or even the several sections of the Church, might exhibit a tendency to throw emphasis on one or another of the elements that made up this deposit of faith that was the common inheritance of all. The East, for instance, laid especial stress on free will: and the West dwelt more pointedly on the ruin of the human race and the absolute need of God's grace for salvation. But neither did the Eastern theologians forget the universal sinfulness and need of redemption, or the necessity, for the realization of that redemption, of God's gracious influences; nor did those of the West deny the self-determination or accountability of men. All the elements of the composite doctrine of man were everywhere confessed; but they were variously emphasized, according to the temper of the writers or the controversial demands of the times. Such a state of affairs, however, was an invitation to heresy, and a prophecy of controversy; just as the simultaneous confession of the unity of God and the Deity of Christ, or of the Deity and the humanity of Christ, inevitably carried in its train a series of heresies and controversies, until the definitions of the doctrines of the Trinity and of the person of Christ were complete. In like manner, it was inevitable that sooner or later some one should arise who would so one-sidedly emphasize one element or the other of the Church's teaching as to salvation, as to throw himself into heresy, and drive the Church, through controversy with him, into a precise definition of the doctrines of free will and grace in their mutual relations.

This new heresiarch came, at the opening of the fifth century, in the person of the British monk, Pelagius. The novelty of the doctrine which he taught is repeatedly asserted by Augustine,[2] and is evident to the historian; but it consisted not in the emphasis that he laid on free will, but rather in the fact that, in emphasizing free will, he denied the ruin of the race and the necessity of grace. This was not only new in Christianity; it was even anti-Christian. Jerome, as well as Augustine, saw this at the time, and speaks of Pelagianism as the 'heresy of Pythagoras and Zeno';[3] and modern writers of the various schools have more or less fully recognized it. Thus Dean Milman thinks that 'the greater part' of Pelagius' letter to Demetrias 'might have been written by an ancient academic';[4] and Bishop Hefele openly declares that their fundamental doctrine, 'that man is virtuous entirely of his own merit, not of the gift of grace,' seems to him 'to be a rehabilitation of the general heathen view of the world,' and compares with it Cicero's words:[5] 'For gold, lands, and all the blessings of life, we have to return thanks to the Gods; but no one ever returned thanks to God for virtue.'[6] The struggle with Pelagianism was thus in reality a struggle for the very foundations of Christianity; and even more dangerously than in the previous theological and Christological controversies, here the practical substance of Christianity was in jeopardy. The real question at issue was whether there was any need for Christianity at all; whether by his own power man might not attain eternal felicity; whether the function of Christianity was to save, or only to render an eternity of happiness more easily attainable by man.[7]

Genetically speaking, Pelagianism was the daughter of legalism; but when it itself conceived, it brought forth an essential deism. It is not without significance that its originators were 'a certain sort of monks;' that is, laymen of ascetic life. From this point of view the Divine law is looked upon as a collection of separate commandments, moral perfection as a simple complex of separate virtues, and a distinct value as a meritorious demand on Divine approbation is ascribed to each good work or attainment in the exercises of piety. It was because this was essentially his point of view that Pelagius could regard man's powers as sufficient to the attainment of sanctity — nay, that he could even assert it to be possible for a man to do more than was required of him. But this involved an essentially deistic conception of man's relations to his Maker. God had endowed His creature with a capacity (possibilitas) or ability (posse) for action, and it was for him to use it. Man was thus a machine, which, just because it was well made, needed no Divine interference for its right working; and the Creator, having once framed him, and endowed him with the posse, henceforth leaves the velle and the esse to him.

At this point we have touched the central and formative principle of Pelagianism. It lies in the assumption of the plenary ability of man; his ability to do all that righteousness can demand — to work out not only his own salvation, but also his own perfection. This is the core of the whole theory; and all the other postulates not only depend upon it, but arise out of it. Both chronologically and logically this is the root of the system.

When we first hear of Pelagius, he is already advanced in years, living in Rome in the odour of sanctity,[8] and enjoying a well-deserved reputation for zeal in exhorting others to a good life, which grew especially warm against those who endeavoured to shelter themselves, when charged with their sins, behind the weakness of nature.[9] He was outraged by the universal excuses on such occasions — 'It is hard!' 'it is difficult!' 'we are not able!' 'we are men!' — 'Oh, blind madness!' he cried: 'we accuse God of a twofold ignorance — that He does not seem to know what He has made, nor what He has commanded — as if forgetting the human weakness of which He is Himself the Author, He has imposed laws on man which He cannot endure.'[10] He himself tells us[11] to that it was his custom, therefore, whenever he had to speak on moral improvement and the conduct of a holy life, to begin by pointing out the power and quality of human nature, and by showing what it was capable of doing. For (he says) he esteemed it of small use to exhort men to what they deemed impossible: hope must rather be our companion, and all longing and effort die when we despair of attaining. So exceedingly ardent an advocate was he of man's unaided ability to do all that God commanded, that when Augustine's noble and entirely scriptural prayer — 'Give what Thou commandest, and command what Thou wilt' — was repeated in his hearing, he was unable to endure it; and somewhat inconsistently contradicted it with such violence as almost to become involved in a strife.[12]

The powers of man, he held, were gifts of God; and it was, therefore, a reproach against Him as if He had made man ill or evil, to believe that they were insufficient for the keeping of His law. Nay, do what we will, we cannot rid ourselves of their sufficiency: 'whether we will, or whether we will not, we have the capacity of not sinning.'13 'I say,' he says, 'that man is able to be without sin, and that he is able to keep the commandments of God;' and this sufficiently direct statement of human ability is in reality the hinge of his whole system.

There were three specially important corollaries which flowed from this assertion of human ability, and Augustine himself recognized these as the chief elements of the system.14 It would be inexplicable on such an assumption, if no man had ever used his ability in keeping God's law; and Pelagius consistently asserted not only that all might be sinless if they chose, but also that many saints, even before Christ, had actually lived free from sin. Again, it follows from man's inalienable ability to be free from sin, that each man comes into the world without entailment of sin or moral weakness from the past acts of men; and Pelagius consistently denied the whole doctrine of original sin. And still again, it follows from the same assumption of ability that man has no need of supernatural assistance in his striving to obey righteousness; and Pelagius consistently denied both the need and reality of divine grace in the sense of an inward help (and especially of a prevenient help) to man's weakness.

It was upon this last point that the greatest stress was laid in the controversy, and Augustine was most of all disturbed that thus God's grace was denied and opposed. No doubt the Pelagians spoke constantly of 'grace,' but they meant by this the primal endowment of man with free will, and the subsequent aid given him in order to its proper use by the revelation of the law and the teaching of the gospel, and, above all, by the forgiveness of past sins in Christ and by Christ's holy example.15 Anything further than this external help they utterly denied; and they denied that this external help itself was absolutely necessary, affirming that it only rendered it easier for man to do what otherwise he had plenary ability for doing. Chronologically, this contention seems to have preceded the assertion which must logically lie at its base, of the freedom of man from any taint, corruption, or weakness due to sin. It was in order that they might deny that man needed help, that they denied that Adam's sin had any further effect on his posterity than might arise from his bad example.

'Before the action of his own proper will,' said Pelagius plainly, 'that only is in man which God made.'16 'As we are procreated without virtue,' he said, 'so also without vice.'17 In a word, 'Nothing that is good and evil, on account of which we are either praiseworthy or blameworthy, is born with us — it is rather done by us; for we are born with capacity for either, but provided with neither.'18 So his later follower, Julian, plainly asserts his 'faith that God creates men obnoxious to no sin, but full of natural innocence, and with capacity for voluntary virtues.'19 So intrenched is free will in nature, that, according to Julian, it is 'just as complete after sins as it was before sins;'20 and what this means may be gathered from Pelagius' definition in the 'Confession of Faith,' that he sent to Innocent: 'We say that man is always able both to sin and not to sin, so as that we may confess that we have free will.' That sin in such circumstances was so common as to be well-nigh universal, was accounted for by the bad example of Adam and the power of habit, the latter being simply the result of imitation of the former. 'Nothing makes well-doing so hard,' writes Pelagius to Demetrias, 'as the long custom of sins which begins from childhood and gradually brings us more and more under its power until it seems to have in some degree the force of nature (vim naturae).' He is even ready to allow for the force of habit in a broad way, on the world at large; and so divides all history into progressive periods, marked by God's (external) grace. At first the light of nature was so strong that men by it alone could live in holiness. And it was only when men's manners became corrupt and tarnished nature began to be insufficient for holy living, that by God's grace the Law was given as an addition to mere nature; and by it 'the original lustre was restored to nature after its blush had been impaired.' And so again, after the habit of sinning once more prevailed among men, and 'the law became unequal to the task of curing it,'21 Christ was given, furnishing men with forgiveness of sins, exhortations to imitation of the example and the holy example itself.22 But though thus a progressive deterioration was confessed, and such a deterioration as rendered desirable at least two supernatural interpositions (in the giving of the law and the coming of Christ), yet no corruption of nature, even by growing habit, is really allowed. It was only an ever-increasing facility in imitating vice which arose from so long a schooling in evil; and all that was needed to rescue men from it was a new explanation of what was right (in the law), or, at the most, the encouragement of forgiveness for what was already done, and a holy example (in Christ) for imitation. Pelagius still asserted our continuous possession of 'a free will which is unimpaired for sinning and for not sinning;' and Julian, that 'our free will is just as full after sins as it was before sins;' although Augustine does not fail to twit him with a charge of inconsistency.23

The peculiar individualism of the Pelagian view of the world comes out strongly in their failure to perceive the effect of habit on nature itself. Just as they conceived of virtue as a complex of virtuous acts, so they conceived of sin exclusively as an act, or series of disconnected acts. They appear not to have risen above the essentially heathen view which had no notion of holiness apart from a series of acts of holiness, or of sin apart from a like series of sinful acts.24 Thus the will was isolated from its acts, and the acts from each other, and all organic connection or continuity of life was not only overlooked but denied.25 After each act of the will, man stood exactly where he did before: indeed, this conception scarcely allows for the existence of a 'man' — only a willing machine is left, at each click of the action of which the spring regains its original position, and is equally ready as before to reperform its function. In such a conception there was no place for character: freedom of will was all. Thus it was not an unnatural mistake which they made, when they forgot the man altogether, and attributed to the faculty of free will, under the name of 'possibilitas' or 'posse,' the ability that belonged rather to the man whose faculty it is, and who is properly responsible for the use he makes of it. Here lies the essential error of their doctrine of free will: they looked upon freedom in its form only, and not in its matter; and, keeping man in perpetual and hopeless equilibrium between good and evil, they permitted no growth of character and no advantage to himself to be gained by man in his successive choices of good. It need not surprise us that the type of thought which thus dissolved the organism of the man into a congeries of disconnected voluntary acts, failed to comprehend the solidarity of the race. To the Pelagian, Adam was a man, nothing more; and it was simply unthinkable that any act of his that left his own subsequent acts uncommitted, could entail sin and guilt upon other men. The same alembic that dissolved the individual into a succession of voluntary acts, could not fail to separate the race into a heap of unconnected units. If sin, as Julian declared, is nothing but will, and the will itself remained intact after each act, how could the individual act of an individual will condition the acts of men as yet unborn? By 'imitation' of his act alone could (under such a conception) other men be affected. And this carried with it the corresponding view of man's relation to Christ. He could forgive us the sins we had committed; He could teach us the true way; He could set us a holy example; and He could exhort us to its imitation. But He could not touch us to enable us to will the good, without destroying the absolute equilibrium of the will between good and evil; and to destroy this was to destroy its freedom, which was the crowning good of our divinely created nature. Surely the Pelagians forgot that man was not made for will, but will for man.

In defending their theory, as we are told by Augustine, there were five claims that they especially made for it.26 It allowed them to praise as was their due, the creature that God had made, the marriage that He had instituted, the law that He had given, the free will which was His greatest endowment to man, and the saints who had followed His counsels. By this they meant that they proclaimed the sinless perfection of human nature in every man as he was brought into the world, and opposed this to the doctrine of original sin; the purity and holiness of marriage and the sexual appetites, and opposed this to the doctrine of the transmission of sin; the ability of the law, as well as and apart from the gospel, to bring men into eternal life, and opposed this to the necessity of inner grace; the integrity of free will to choose the good, and opposed this to the necessity of divine aid; and the perfection of the lives of the saints, and opposed this to the doctrine of universal sinfulness. Other questions, concerning the origin of souls, the necessity of baptism for infants, the original immortality of Adam, lay more on the skirts of the controversy, and were rather consequences of their teaching than parts of it. As it was an obvious fact that all men died, they could not admit that Adam's death was a consequence of sin lest they should be forced to confess that his sin had injured all men; they therefore asserted that physical death belonged to the very nature of man, and that Adam would have died even had he not sinned.27 So, as it was impossible to deny that the Church everywhere baptized infants, they could not refuse them baptism without confessing themselves innovators in doctrine; and therefore they contended that infants were not baptized for forgiveness of sins, but in order to attain a higher state of salvation. Finally, they conceived that if it was admitted that souls were directly created by God for each birth, it could not be asserted that they came into the world soiled by sin and under condemnation; and therefore they loudly championed this theory of the origin of souls.

The teachings of the Pelagians, it will be readily seen, easily welded themselves into a system, the essential and formative elements of which were entirely new in the Christian Church; and this startlingly new reading of man's condition, powers, and dependence for salvation, it was, that broke like a thunderbolt upon the Western Church at the opening of the fifth century, and forced her to reconsider, from the foundations, her whole teaching as to man and his salvation.

Part Two - The External History of the Pelagian Controversy

Pelagius seems to have been already somewhat softened by increasing age when he came to Rome about the opening of the fifth century. He was also constitutionally averse to controversy; and although in his zeal for Christian morals, and in his conviction that no man would attempt to do what he was not persuaded he had natural power to perform, he diligently propagated his doctrines privately, he was careful to rouse no opposition, and was content to make what progress he could quietly and without open discussion. His methods of work sufficiently appear in the pages of his 'Commentary on the Epistles of Saint Paul,' which was written and published during these years, and which exhibits learning and a sober and correct but somewhat shallow exegetical skill. In this work, he manages to give expression to all the main elements of his system, but always introduces them indirectly, not as the true exegesis, but by way of objections to the ordinary teaching, which were in need of discussion. The most important fruit of his residence in Rome was the conversion to his views of the Advocate Coelestius, who brought the courage of youth and the argumentative training of a lawyer to the propagation of the new teaching. It was through him that it first broke out into public controversy, and received its first ecclesiastical examination and rejection. Fleeing from Alaric's second raid on Rome, the two friends landed together in Africa (A.D. 411), whence Pelagius soon afterwards departed for Palestine, leaving the bolder and more contentious Coelestius behind at Carthage. Here Coelestius sought ordination as a presbyter. But the Milanese deacon Paulinus stood forward in accusation of him as a heretic, and the matter was brought before a synod under the presidency of Bishop Aurelius.

Paulinus' charge consisted of seven items, which asserted that Coelestius taught the following heresies: that Adam was made mortal, and would have died, whether he sinned or did not sin; that the sin of Adam injured himself alone, not the human race; that new-born children are in that state in which Adam was before his sin; that the whole human race does not, on the one hand, die on account of the death or the fall of Adam, nor, on the other, rise again on account of the resurrection of Christ; that infants, even though not baptized, have eternal life; that the law leads to the kingdom of heaven in the same way as the gospel; and that, even before the Lord's coming, there had been men without sin. Only two fragments of the proceedings of the synod in investigating this charge have come down to us; but it is easy to see that Coelestius was contumacious, and refused to reject any of the propositions charged against him, except the one which had reference to the salvation of infants that die unbaptized—the sole one that admitted of sound defence. As touching the transmission of sin, he would only say that it was an open question in the Church, and that he had heard both opinions from Church dignitaries; so that the subject needed investigation, and should not be made the ground for a charge of heresy. The natural result was, that, on refusing to condemn the propositions charged against him, he was himself condemned and excommunicated by the synod. Soon afterwards he sailed to Ephesus, where he obtained the ordination which he sought.

Meanwhile Pelagius was living quietly in Palestine, whither in the summer of 415 a young Spanish presbyter, Paulus Orosius by name, came with letters from Augustine to Jerome, and was invited, near the end of July in that year, to a diocesan synod, presided over by John of Jerusalem. There he was asked about Pelagius and Coelestius, and proceeded to give an account of the condemnation of the latter at the synod of Carthage, and of Augustine's literary refutation of the former. Pelagius was sent for, and the proceedings became an examination into his teachings. The chief matter brought up was his assertion of the possibility of men living sinlessly in this world; but the favour of the bishop towards him, the intemperance of Orosius, and the difficulty of communication between the parties arising from difference of language, combined so to clog proceedings that nothing was done; and the whole matter, as Western in its origin, was referred to the Bishop of Rome for examination and decision.

Soon afterwards two Gallic bishops—Heros of Arles, and Lazarus of Aix—who were then in Palestine, lodged a formal accusation against Pelagius with the metropolitan, Eulogius of Caesarea; and he convened a synod of fourteen bishops which met at Lydda (Diospolis), in December of the same year (415), for the trial of the case. Perhaps no greater ecclesiastical farce was ever enacted than this synod exhibited. When the time arrived, the accusers were prevented from being present by illness, and Pelagius was confronted only by the written accusation. This was both unskilfully drawn, and was written in Latin which the synod did not understand. It was, therefore, not even consecutively read, and was only head by head rendered into Greek by an interpreter. Pelagius began by reading aloud several letters to himself from various men of reputation in the Episcopate—among them a friendly note from Augustine. Thoroughly acquainted with both Latin and Greek, he was enabled skillfully to thread every difficulty, and pass safely through the ordeal. Jerome called this a 'miserable synod,' and not unjustly: at the same time it is sufficient to vindicate the honesty and earnestness of the bishops' intentions, that even in such circumstances, and despite the more undeveloped opinions of the East on the questions involved, Pelagius escaped condemnation only by a course of most ingenious disingenuousness, and only at the cost both of disowning Coelestius and his teachings, of which he had been the real father, and of leading the synod to believe that he was anathematizing the very doctrines which he was himself proclaiming. There is really no possibility of doubting, as any one will see who reads the proceedings of the synod, that Pelagius obtained his acquittal here either by a 'lying condemnation or a tricky interpretation' of his own teachings; and Augustine is perfectly justified in asserting that the 'heresy was not acquitted, but the man who denied the heresy,' and who would himself have been anathematized had he not anathematized the heresy.

However obtained, the acquittal of Pelagius was yet an accomplished fact. Neither he nor his friends delayed to make the most widely extended use of their good fortune. Pelagius himself was jubilant. Accounts of the synodal proceedings were sent to the West, not altogether free from uncandid alterations; and Pelagius soon put forth a work In Defence of Free-Will, in which he triumphed in his acquittal and 'explained his explanations' at the synod. Nor were the champions of the opposite opinion idle. As soon as the news arrived in North Africa, and before the authentic records of the synod had reached that region, the condemnation of Pelagius and Coelestius was re-affirmed in two provincial synods—one, consisting of sixty-eight bishops, met at Carthage about midsummer of 416; and the other, consisting of about sixty bishops, met soon afterwards at Mileve (Mila). Thus Palestine and North Africa were arrayed against one another, and it became of great importance to obtain the support of the Patriarchal See of Rome. Both sides made the attempt, but fortune favored the Africans. Each of the North-African synods sent a synodal letter to Innocent I., then Bishop of Rome, engaging his assent to their action: to these, five bishops, Aurelius of Carthage and Augustine among them, added a third 'familiar' letter of their own, in which they urged upon Innocent to examine into Pelagius' teaching, and provided him with the material on which he might base a decision. The letters reached Innocent in time for him to take advice of his clergy, and send favorable replies on Jan. 27, 417. In these he expressed his agreement with the African decisions, asserted the necessity of inward grace, rejected the Pelagian theory of infant baptism, and declared Pelagius and Coelestius excommunicated until they should return to orthodoxy. In about six weeks more he was dead: but Zosimus, his successor, was scarcely installed in his place before Coelestius appeared at Rome in person to plead his cause; while shortly afterwards letters arrived from Pelagius addressed to Innocent, and by an artful statement of his belief and a recommendation from Praylus, lately become bishop of Jerusalem in John's stead, attempting to enlist Rome in his favour. Zosimus, who appears to have been a Greek and therefore inclined to make little of the merits of this Western controversy, went over to Coelestius at once, upon his profession of willingness to anathematize all doctrines which the pontifical see had condemned or should condemn; and wrote a sharp and arrogant letter to Africa, proclaiming Coelestius 'catholic,' and requiring the Africans to appear within two months at Rome to prosecute their charges, or else to abandon them. On the arrival of Pelagius' papers, this letter was followed by another (September, 417), in which Zosimus, with the approbation of the clergy, declared both Pelagius and Coelestius to be orthodox, and severely rebuked the Africans for their hasty judgment. It is difficult to understand Zosimus' action in this matter: neither of the confessions presented by the accused teachers ought to have deceived him, and if he was seizing the occasion to magnify the Roman see, his mistake was dreadful. Late in 417, or early in 418, the African bishops assembled at Carthage, in number more than two hundred, and replied to Zosimus that they had decided that the sentence pronounced against Pelagius and Coelestius should remain in force until they should unequivocally acknowledge that 'we are aided by the grace of God, through Christ, not only to know, but to do what is right, in each single act, so that without grace we are unable to have, think, speak, or do anything pertaining to piety.' This firmness made Zosimus waver. He answered swellingly but timidly, declaring that he had maturely examined the matter, but it had not been his intention finally to acquit Coelestius; and now he had left all things in the condition in which they were before, but he claimed the right of final judgment to himself. Matters were hastening to a conclusion, however, that would leave him no opportunity to escape from the mortification of an entire change of front. This letter was written on the 21st of March, 418; it was received in Africa on the 29th of April; and on the very next day an imperial decree was issued from Ravenna ordering Pelagius and Coelestius to be banished from Rome, with all who held their opinions; while on the next day, May 1, a plenary council of about two hundred bishops met at Carthage, and in nine canons condemned all the essential features of Pelagianism. Whether this simultaneous action was the result of skillful arrangement, can only be conjectured: its effect was in any case necessarily crushing. There could be no appeal from the civil decision, and it played directly into the hands of the African definition of the faith. The synod's nine canons part naturally into three triads. The first of these deals with the relation of mankind to original sin, and anathematizes in turn those who assert that physical death is a necessity of nature, and not a result of Adam's sin; those who assert that new-born children derive nothing of original sin from Adam to be expiated by the laver of regeneration; and those who assert a distinction between the kingdom of heaven and eternal life, for entrance into the former of which alone baptism is necessary. The second triad deals with the nature of grace, and anathematizes those who assert that grace brings only remission of past sins, not aid in avoiding future ones; those who assert that grace aids us not to sin, only by teaching us what is sinful, not by enabling us to will and do what we know to be right; and those who assert that grace only enables us to do more easily what we should without it still be able to do. The third triad deals with the universal sinfulness of the race, and anathematizes those who assert that the apostles' (I John i. 8) confession of sin is due only to their humility; those who say that 'Forgive us our trespasses' in the Lord's Prayer, is pronounced by the saints, not for themselves, but for the sinners in their company; and those who say that the saints use these words of themselves only out of humility and not truly. Here we see a careful traversing of the whole ground of the controversy, with a conscious reference to the three chief contentions of the Pelagian teachers.

The appeal to the civil power, by whomsoever made, was, of course, indefensible, although it accorded with the opinions of the day, and was entirely approved by Augustine. But it was the ruin of the Pelagian cause. Zosimus found himself forced either to go into banishment with his wards, or to desert their cause. He appears never to have had any personal convictions on the dogmatic points involved in the controversy, and so, all the more readily, yielded to the necessity of the moment. He cited Coelestius to appear before a council for a new examination; but that heresiarch consulted prudence, and withdrew from the city. Zosimus, possibly in the effort to appear a leader in the cause he had opposed, not only condemned and excommunicated the men whom less than six months before he had pronounced 'orthodox' after a `mature consideration of the matters involved,' but, in obedience to the imperial decree, issued a stringent paper which condemned Pelagius and the Pelagians, and affirmed the African doctrines as to corruption of nature, true grace, and the necessity of baptism. To this he required subscription from all bishops as a test of orthodoxy. Eighteen Italian bishops refused their signature, with Julian of Eclanum, henceforth to be the champion of the Pelagian party, at their head, and were therefore deposed, although several of them afterwards recanted, and were restored. In Julian, the heresy obtained an advocate, who, if aught could have been done for its re-instatement, would surely have proved successful. He was the boldest, the strongest, at once the most acute and the most weighty, of all the disputants of his party. But the ecclesiastical standing of this heresy was already determined. The policy of Zosimus' test act was imposed by imperial authority on North Africa in 419. The exiled bishops were driven from Constantinople by Atticus in 424; and they are said to have been condemned at a Cilician synod in 423, and at an Antiochian one in 424. Thus the East itself was preparing for the final act in the drama. The exiled bishops were with Nestorius at Constantinople in 429; and that patriarch unsuccessfully interceded for them with Coelestine, then Bishop of Rome. The conjunction was ominous. And at the ecumenical synod at Ephesus in 431, we again find the 'Coelestians' side by side with Nestorius, sharers in his condemnation.

But Pelagianism did not so die as not to leave a legacy behind it. 'Remainders of Pelagianism' soon showed themselves in Southern Gaul, where a body of monastic leaders attempted to find a middle ground on which they could stand, by allowing the Augustineian doctrine of assisting grace, but retaining the Pelagian conception of our self-determination to good. We first hear of them in 428, through letters from two laymen, Prosper and Hilary, to Augustine, as men who accepted original sin and the necessity of grace, but asserted that men began their turning to God, and God helped their beginning. They taught that all men are sinners, and that they derive their sin from Adam; that they can by no means save themselves, but need God's assisting grace; and that this grace is gratuitous in the sense that men cannot really deserve it, and yet that it is not irresistible, nor given always without the occasion of its gift having been determined by men's attitude towards God; so that, though not given on account of the merits of men, it is given according to those merits, actual or foreseen. The leader of this new movement was John Cassian, a pupil of Chrysostom (to whom he attributed all that was good in his life and will), and the fountain-head of Gallic monasticism; and its chief champion at a somewhat later day was Faustus of Rhegium (Riez).

The Augustineian opposition was at first led by the vigorous controversialist, Prosper of Aquitaine, and, in the next century, by the wise, moderate, and good Caesarius of Arles, who brought the contest to a conclusion in the victory of a softened Augustineianism. Already in 431 a letter was obtained from Pope Coelestine, designed to close the controversy in favor of Augustineianism, and in 496 Pope Gelasius condemned the writings of Faustus in the first index of forbidden books; while, near the end of the first quarter of the sixth century, Pope Hormisdas was appealed to for a renewed condemnation. The end was now in sight. The famous second Synod of Orange met under the presidency of Caesarius at that ancient town on the 3d of July, 529, and drew up a series of moderate articles which received the ratification of Boniface II. in the following year. In these articles there is affirmed an anxiously guarded Augustineianism, a somewhat weakened Augustineianism, but yet a distinctive Augustineianism; and, so far as a formal condemnation could reach, semi-Pelagianism was suppressed by them in the whole Western Church. But councils and popes can only decree; and Cassian and Vincent and Faustus, despite Caesarius and Boniface and Gregory, retained an influence among their countrymen which never died away.

Part Three - Augustine's Part in The Controversy

Both by nature and by grace, Augustine was formed to be the champion of truth in this controversy. Of a naturally philosophical temperament, he saw into the springs of life with a vividness of mental perception to which most men are strangers; and his own experiences in his long life of resistance to, and then of yielding to, the drawings of God's grace, gave him a clear apprehension of the great evangelic principle that God seeks men, not men God, such as no sophistry could cloud. However much his philosophy or theology might undergo change in other particulars, there was one conviction too deeply imprinted upon his heart ever to fade or alter—the conviction of the ineffableness of God's grace. Grace—man's absolute dependence on God as the source of all good—this was the common, nay, the formative element, in all stages of his doctrinal development, which was marked only by the ever growing consistency with which he built his theology around this central principle. Already in 397—the year after he became bishop—we find him enunciating with admirable clearness all the essential elements of his teaching, as he afterwards opposed them to Pelagius. It was inevitable, therefore, that although he was rejoiced when he heard, some years later, of the zealous labours of this pious monk in Rome towards stemming the tide of luxury and sin, and esteemed him for his devout life, and loved him for his Christian activity, he yet was deeply troubled when subsequent rumours reached him that he was "disputing against the grace of God." He tells us over and over again, that this was a thing no pious heart could endure; and we perceive that, from this moment, Augustine was only biding his time, and awaiting a fitting opportunity to join issue with the denier of the Holy of holies of his whole, I will not say theology merely, but life. "Although I was grieved by this," he says, "and it was told me by men whom I believed, I yet desired to have something of such sort from his own lips or in some book of his, so that, if I began to refute it, he would not be able to deny it." Thus he actually excuses himself for not entering into the controversy earlier. When Pelagius came to Africa, then, it was almost as if he had deliberately sought his fate. But circumstances secured a lull before the storm. He visited Hippo; but Augustine was absent, although he did not fail to inform himself on his return that Pelagius while there had not been heard to say "anything at all of this kind." The controversy against the Donatists was now occupying all the energies of the African Church, and Augustine himself was a ruling spirit in the great conference now holding at Carthage with them. While there, he was so immersed in this business, that, although he once or twice saw the face of Pelagius, he had no conversation with him; and although his ears were wounded by a casual remark which he heard, to the effect "that infants were not baptized for remission of sins, but for consecration to Christ," he allowed himself to pass over the matter, "because there was no opportunity to contradict it, and those who said it were not such men as could cause him solicitude for their influence."

It appears from these facts, given us by himself, that Augustine was not only ready for, but was looking for, the coming controversy. It can scarcely have been a surprise to him when Paulinus accused Coelestius (412); and, although he was not a member of the council which condemned him, it was inevitable that he should at once take the leading part in the consequent controversy. Coelestius and his friends did not silently submit to the judgment that had been passed upon their teaching: they could not openly propagate their heresy, but they were diligent in spreading their plaints privately and by subterraneous whispers among the people. This was met by the Catholics in public sermons and familiar colloquies held everywhere. But this wise rule was observed—to contend against the erroneous teachings, but to keep silence as to the teachers, that so (as Augustine explains) "the men might rather be brought to see and acknowledge their error through fear of ecclesiastical judgment than be punished by the actual judgment." Augustine was abundant in these oral labours; and many of his sermons directed against Pelagian error have come down to us, although it is often impossible to be sure as to their date. For one of them (170) he took his text from Phil. iii. 6-16, "as touching the righteousness which is by the law blameless; howbeit what things were gain to me, those have I counted loss for Christ." He begins by asking how the apostle could count his blameless conversation according to the righteousness which is from the law as dung and loss, and then proceeds to explain the purpose for which the law was given, our state by nature and under law, and the kind of blamelessness that the law could produce, ending by showing that man can have no righteousness except from God, and no perfect righteousness except in heaven. Three others (174, 175, 176) had as their text I Tim. i. 15, 16, and developed its teaching, that the universal sin of the world and its helplessness in sin constituted the necessity of the incarnation; and especially that the necessity of Christ's grace for salvation was just as great for infants as for adults. Much is very forcibly said in these sermons which was afterwards incorporated in his treatises. "There was no reason," he insists, "for the coming of Christ the Lord except to save sinners. Take away diseases, take away wounds, and there is no reason for medicine. If the great Physician came from heaven, a great sick man was lying ill through the whole world. That sick man is the human race" (175, 1). "He who says, `I am not a sinner,' or `I was not,' is ungrateful to the Saviour. No one of men in that mass of mortals which flows down from Adam, no one at all of men is not sick: no one is healed without the grace of Christ. Why do you ask whether infants are sick from Adam? For they, too, are brought to the church; and, if they cannot run thither on their own feet, they run on the feet of others that they may be healed. Mother Church accommodates others' feet to them so that they may come, others' heart so that they may believe, others' tongue so that they may confess; and, since they are sick by another's sin, so when they are healed they are saved by another's confession in their behalf. Let, then, no one buzz strange doctrines to you. This the Church has always had, has always held; this she has received from the faith of the elders; this she will perseveringly guard until the end. Since the whole have no need of a physician, but only the sick, what need, then, has the infant of Christ, if he is not sick? If he is well, why does he seek the physician through those who love him? If, when infants are brought, they are said to have no sin of inheritance (peccatum propaginis) at all, and yet come to Christ, why is it not said in the church to those that bring them, `take these innocents hence; the physician is not needed by the well, but by the sick; Christ came not to call the just, but sinners'? It never has been said, and it never will be said. Let each one therefore, brethren, speak for him who cannot speak for himself. It is much the custom to intrust the inheritance of orphans to the bishops; how much more the grace of infants! The bishop protects the orphan lest he should be oppressed by strangers, his parents being dead. Let him cry out more for the infant who, he fears, will be slain by his parents. Who comes to Christ has something in him to be healed; and he who has not, has no reason for seeking the physician. Let parents choose one of two things: let them either confess that there is sin to be healed in their infants, or let them cease bringing them to the physician. This is nothing else than to wish to bring a well person to the physician. Why do you bring him? To be baptized. Whom? The infant. To whom do you bring him? To Christ. To Him, of course, who came into the world? Certainly, he says. Why did He come into the world? To save sinners. Then he whom you bring has in him that which needs saving?" So again: "He who says that the age of infancy does not need Jesus' salvation, says nothing else than that the Lord Christ is not Jesus to faithful infants; i.e., to infants baptized in Christ. For what is Jesus? Jesus means saviour. He is not Jesus to those whom He does not save, who do not need to be saved. Now, if your hearts can bear that Christ is not Jesus to any of the baptized, I do not know how you can be acknowledged to have sound faith. They are infants, but they are made members of Him. They are infants, but they receive His sacraments. They are infants, but they become partakers of His table, so that they may have life." The preveniency of grace is explicitly asserted in these sermons. In one he says, "Zaccheus was seen, and saw; but unless he had been seen, he would not have seen. For `whom He predestinated, them also He called.' In order that we may see, we are seen; that we may love, we are loved. `My God, may His pity prevent me!'" And in another, at more length: "His calling has preceded you, so that you may have a good will. Cry out, `My God, let Thy mercy prevent me' (Ps. lviii. 11.). That you may be, that you may feel, that you may hear, that you may consent, His mercy prevents you. It prevents you in all things; and do you too prevent His judgment in something. In what, do you say? In what? In confessing that you have all these things from God, whatever you have of good; and from yourself whatever you have of evil" (176, 5). "We owe therefore to Him that we are, that we are alive, that we understand: that we are men, that we live well, that we understand aright, we owe to Him. Nothing is ours except the sin that we have. For what have we that we did not receive?" (I Cor. ix. 7) (176, 6).

It was not long, however, before the controversy was driven out of the region of sermons into that of regular treatises. The occasion for Augustine's first appearance in a written document bearing on the controversy, was given by certain questions which were sent to him for answer by "the tribune and notary" Marcellinus, with whom he had cemented his intimacy at Carthage, the previous year, when this notable official was presiding, by the emperor's orders, over the great conference of the catholics and Donatists. The mere fact that Marcellinus, still at Carthage, where Coelestius had been brought to trial, wrote to Augustine at Hippo for written answers to important questions connected with the Pelagian heresy, speaks volumes for the prominent position he had already assumed in the controversy. The questions that were sent, concerned the connection of death with sin, the transmission of sin, the possibility of a sinless life, and especially infants' need of baptism. Augustine was immersed in abundant labours when they reached him: but he could not resist this appeal, and that the less as the Pelagian controversy had already grown to a place of the first importance in his eyes. The result was his treatise, On the Merits and Remission of Sins and on the Baptism of Infants, consisting of two books, and written in 412. The first book of this work is an argument for original sin, drawn from the universal reign of death in the world (2-8), from the teaching of Rom. v. 12-21 (9-20), and chiefly from the baptism of infants (21-70). It opens by exploding the Pelagian contention that death is of nature, and Adam would have died even had he not sinned, by showing that the penalty threatened to Adam included physical death (Gen. iii. 19), and that it is due to him that we all die (Rom. viii. 10, 11; I Cor. xv. 21) (2-8). Then the Pelagian assertion that we are injured in Adam's sin only by its bad example, which we imitate, not by any propagation from it, is tested by an exposition of Rom. v. 12 sq. (9-20). And then the main subject of the book is reached, and the writer sharply presses the Pelagians with the universal and primeval fact of the baptism of infants, as a proof of original sin (21-70). He tracks out all their subterfuges—showing the absurdity of the assertions that infants are baptized for the remission of sins that they have themselves committed since birth (22), or in order to obtain a higher stage of salvation (23-28), or because of sin committed in some previous state of existence (31-33). Then turning to the positive side, he shows at length that the Scriptures teach that Christ came to save sinners, that baptism is for the remission of sins, and that all that partake of it are confessedly sinners (34 sq.); then he points out that John ii. 7, 8, on which the Pelagians relied, cannot be held to distinguish between ordinary salvation and a higher form, under the name of "the kingdom of God" (58 sq.); and he closes by showing that the very manner in which baptism was administered, with its exorcism and exsufflation, implied the infant to be a sinner (63), and by suggesting that the peculiar helplessness of infancy, so different not only from the earliest age of Adam, but also from that of many young animals, may possibly be itself penal (64-69). The second book treats, with similar fulness, the question of the perfection of human righteousness in this life. After an exordium which speaks of the will and its limitations, and of the need of God's assisting grace (1-6), the writer raises four questions. First, whether it may be said to be possible, by God's grace, for a man to attain a condition of entire sinlessness in this life (7). This he answers in the affirmative. Secondly, he asks, whether any one has ever done this, or may ever be expected to do it, and answers in the negative on the testimony of Scripture (8-25). Thirdly, he asks why not, and replies briefly because men are unwilling, explaining at length what he means by this (26-33). Finally, he inquires whether any man has ever existed, exists now, or will ever exist, entirely without sin—this question differing from the second inasmuch as that asked after the attainment in this life of a state in which sinning should cease, while this seeks a man who has never been guilty of sin, implying the absence of original as well as of actual sin. After answering this in the negative (34), Augustine discusses anew the question of original sin. Here after expounding from the positive side (35-38) the condition of man in paradise, the nature of his probation, and of the fall and its effects both on him and his posterity, and the kind of redemption that has been provided in the incarnation, he proceeds to answer certain cavils (39 sq.), such as, "Why should children of baptized people need baptism?"-"How can a sin be remitted to the father and held against the child?"-"If physical death comes from Adam, ought we not to be released from it on believing in Christ?"-and concludes with an exhortation to hold fast to the exact truth, turning neither to the right nor left—neither saying that we have no sin, nor surrendering ourselves to our sin (57 sq.).

After these books were completed, Augustine came into possession of Pelagius' Commentary on Paul's Epistles , which was written while he was living in Rome (before 410), and found it to contain some arguments that he had not treated—such arguments, he tells us, as he had not imagined could be held by any one. Unwilling to re-open his finished argument, he now began a long supplementary letter to Marcellinus, which he intended to serve as a third and concluding book to his work. He was some time in completing this letter. He had asked to have the former two books returned to him; and it is a curious indication of his overworked state of mind, that he forgot what he wanted with them: he visited Carthage while the letter was in hand, and saw Marcellinus personally; and even after his return to Hippo, it dragged along, amid many distractions, slowly towards completion. Meanwhile, a long letter was written to Honoratus, in which a section on the grace of the New Testament was incorporated. At length the promised supplement was completed. It was professedly a criticism of Pelagius' Commentary, and therefore naturally mentioned his name; but Augustine even goes out of his way to speak as highly of his opponent as he can, -although it is apparent that his esteem is not very high for his strength of mind, and is even less high for the moral quality that led to his odd, oblique way of expressing his opinions. There is even a half sarcasm in the way he speaks of Pelagius' care and circumspection, which was certainly justified by the event. The letter opens by stating and criticising in a very acute and telling dialectic, the new arguments of Pelagius, which were such as the following: "If Adam's sin injured even those who do not sin, Christ's righteousness ought likewise to profit even those who do not believe" (2-4); "No man can transmit what he has not; and hence, if baptism cleanses from sin, the children of baptized parents ought to be free from sin;" "God remits one's own sins, and can scarcely, therefore, impute another's to us; and if the soul is created, it would certainly be unjust to impute Adam's alien sin to it" (5). The stress of the letter, however, is laid upon two contentions—1. That whatever else may be ambiguous in the Scriptures, they are perfectly clear that no man can have eternal life except in Christ, who came to call sinners to repentance (7); and 2. That original sin in infants has always been, in the Church, one of the fixed facts, to be used as a basis of argument, in order to reach the truth in other matters, and has never itself been called in question before (10-14). At this point, the writer returns to the second and third of the new arguments of Pelagius mentioned above, and discusses them more fully (15-20), closing with a recapitulation of the three great points that had been raised; viz., that both death and sin are derived from Adam's sin by all his posterity; that infants need salvation, and hence baptism; and that no man ever attains in this life such a state of holiness that he cannot truly pray, "Forgive us our trespasses."

Augustine was now to learn that one service often entails another. Marcellinus wrote to say that he was puzzled by what had been said in the second book of this work, as to the possibility of man's attaining to sinlessness in this life, while yet it was asserted that no man ever had attained, or ever would attain, it. How, he asked, can that be said to be possible which is, and which will remain, unexampled? In reply, Augustine wrote, during this same year (412), and sent to his noble friend, another work, which he calls On the Spirit and the Letter, from the prominence which he gives in it to the words of 2 Cor. iii. 6. He did not content himself with a simple, direct answer to Marcellinus' question, but goes at length into a profound disquisition into the roots of the doctrine, and thus gives us, not a mere explanation of a former contention, but a new treatise on a new subject—the absolute necessity of the grace of God for any good living. He begins by explaining to Marcellinus that he has affirmed the possibility while denying the actuality of a sinless life, on the ground that all things are possible to God—even the passage of a camel through the eye of a needle, which nevertheless has never occurred (1, 2). For, in speaking of man's perfection, we are speaking really of a work of God—and one which is none the less His work because it is wrought through the instrumentality of man, and in the use of his free will. The Scriptures, indeed, teach that no man lives without sin, but this is only the proclamation of a matter of fact; and although it is thus contrary to fact and Scripture to assert that men may be found that live sinlessly, yet such an assertion would not be fatal heresy. What is unbearable, is that men should assert it to be possible for man, unaided by God, to attain this perfection. This is to speak against the grace of God: it is to put in man's power what is only possible to the almighty grace of God (3, 4). No doubt, even these men do not, in so many words, exclude the aid of grace in perfecting human life—they affirm God's help; but they make it consist in His gift to man of a perfectly free will, and in His addition to this of commandments and teachings which make known to him what he is to seek and what to avoid, and so enable him to direct his free will to what is good. What, however, does such a "grace" amount to? (5). Man needs something more than to know the right way: he needs to love it, or he will not walk in it; and all mere teaching, which can do nothing more than bring us knowledge of what we ought to do, is but the letter that killeth. What we need is some inward, Spirit-given aid to the keeping of what by the law we know ought to be kept. Mere knowledge slays: while to lead a holy life is the gift of God—not only because He has given us will, nor only because He has taught us the right way, but because by the Holy Spirit He sheds love abroad in the hearts of all those whom He has predestinated, and will call and justify and glorify (Rom. viii. 29, 30). To prove this, he states to be the object of the present treatise; and after investigating the meaning of 2 Cor. iii. 6, and showing that "the letter" there means the law as a system of precepts, which reveals sin rather than takes it away, points out the way rather than gives strength to walk in it, and therefore slays the soul by shutting it up under sin—while "the Spirit" is God's Holy Ghost who is shed abroad in our hearts to give us strength to walk aright—he undertakes to prove this position from the teachings of the Epistle to the Romans at large. This contention, it will be seen, cut at the very roots of Pelagianism: if all mere teaching slays the soul, as Paul asserts, then all that what they called "grace" could, when alone, do, was to destroy; and the upshot of "helping" man by simply giving him free will, and pointing out the way to him, would be the loss of the whole race. Not that the law is sin: Augustine teaches that it is holy and good, and God's instrument in salvation. Not that free will is done away: it is by free will that men are led into holiness. But the purpose of the law (he teaches) is to make men so feel their lost estate as to seek the help by which alone they may be saved; and will is only then liberated to do good when grace has made it free. "What the law of works enjoins by menace, that the law of faith secures by faith. What the law of works does is to say, `Do what I command thee;' but by the law of faith we say to God, `Give me what thou commandest.' "(22). In the midst of this argument, Augustine is led to discuss the differentiating characteristics of the Old and New Testaments; and he expounds at length (33-42) the passage in Jer. xxxi. 31-34, showing that, in the prophet's view, the difference between the two covenants is that in the Old, the law is an external thing written on stones; while in the New, it is written internally on the heart, so that men now wish to do what the law prescribes. This writing on the heart is nothing else, he explains, than the shedding abroad by the Holy Spirit of love in our hearts, so that we love God's will, and therefore freely do it. Towards the end of the treatise (50-61), he treats in an absorbingly interesting way of the mutual relations of free will, faith, and grace, contending that all co-exist without the voiding of any. It is by free will that we believe; but it is only as grace moves us, that we are able to use our free will for believing; and it is only after we are thus led by grace to believe, that we obtain all other goods. In prosecuting this analysis, Augustine is led to distinguish very sharply between the faculty and use of free will (58), as well as between ability and volition (53). Faith is an act of the man himself; but only as he is given the power from on high to will to believe, will he believe (57, 60).

By this work, Augustine completed, in his treatment of Pelagianism, the circle of that triad of doctrines which he himself looked upon as most endangered by this heresy, - original sin, the imperfection of human righteousness, the necessity of grace. In his mind, the last was the kernel of the whole controversy; and this was a subject which he could never approach without some heightened fervour. This accounts for the great attractiveness of the present work—through the whole fabric of which runs the golden thread of the praise of God's ineffable grace. In Canon Bright's opinion, it "perhaps, next to the 'Confessions,' tells us most of the thoughts of that 'rich, profound, and affectionate mind' on the soul's relations to its God."

After the publication of these treatises, the controversy certainly did not lull; but it relapsed for nearly three years again, into less public courses. Meanwhile, Augustine was busy, among other most distracting cares (Ep. 145, 1), still defending the grace of God, by letters and sermons. A fair illustration of his state of mind at this time, may be obtained from his letter to Anastasius (145), which assuredly must have been written soon after the treatise On the Spirit and the Letter. Throughout this letter, there are adumbrations of the same train of thought that filled this treatise; and there is one passage which may almost be taken as a summary of it. Augustine is so weary of the vexatious cares that filled his life, that he is ready to long for the everlasting rest, and yet bewails the weakness which allowed the sweetness of external things still to insinuate itself into his heart. Victory over, and emancipation from, this, he asserts, "cannot, without God's grace, be achieved by the human will, which is by no means to be called free so long as it is subject to enslaving lusts." Then he proceeds: "The law, therefore, by teaching and commanding what cannot be fulfilled without grace, demonstrates to man his weakness, in order that the weakness, thus proved, may resort to the Saviour, by whose healing the will may be able to do what it found impossible in its weakness. So, then, the law brings us to faith, faith obtains the Spirit in fuller measure, the Spirit sheds love abroad in us, and love fulfils the law. For this reason the law is called a schoolmaster, under whose threatening and severity 'whosoever shall call on the name of the Lord shall be delivered.' But 'how shall they call on Him in whom they have not believed?' Wherefore, that the letter without the Spirit may not kill, the life-giving Spirit is given to those that believe and call upon Him; but the love of God is poured out into our hearts by the Holy Spirit who is given to us, so that the words of the same apostle, 'Love is the fulfilling of the law,' may be realized. Thus the law is good to him that uses it lawfully; and he uses it lawfully, who, understanding wherefore it was given, betakes himself, under the pressure of its threatening, to liberating grace. Whoever ungratefully despises this grace by which the ungodly is justified, and trusts in his own strength for fulfilling the law, being ignorant of God's righteousness, and going about to establish his own righteousness, is not submitting himself to the righteousness of God; and therefore the law is made to him not a help to pardon, but the bond of guilt; not because the law is evil, but because 'sin,' as it is written, 'works death to such persons by that which is good.' For by the commandment, he sins more grievously, who, by the commandment, knows how evil are the sins which he commits." Although Augustine states clearly that this letter is written against those "who arrogate too much to the human will, imagining that, the law being given, the will is, of its own strength, sufficient to fulfil the law, though not assisted by any grace imparted by the Holy Ghost, in addition to instruction in the law,"-he refrains still from mentioning the names of the authors of this teaching, evidently out of a lingering tenderness in his treatment of them. This will help us to explain the courtesy of a note which he sent to Pelagius himself at about this time, in reply to a letter he had received some time before from him; of which Pelagius afterwards (at the Synod of Diospolis) made, to say the least of it, an ungenerous use. This note, Augustine tells us, was written with "tempered praises" (wherefrom we see his lessening respect for the man), and so as to admonish Pelagius to think rightly concerning grace—so far as could be done without raising the dregs of the controversy in a formal note. This he accomplished by praying from the Lord for him, those good things by which he might be good forever, and might live eternally with

Him who is eternal; and by asking his prayers in return, that he, too, might be made by the Lord such as he seemed to suppose he already was. How Augustine could really intend these prayers to be understood as an admonition to Pelagius to look to God for what he was seeking to work out for himself, is fully illustrated by the closing words of this almost contemporary letter to Anastasius: "Pray, therefore, for us," he writes, "that we may be righteous—an attainment wholly beyond a man's reach, unless he know righteousness, and be willing to practise it, but one which is immediately realized when he is perfectly willing; but this cannot be in him unless he is healed by the grace of the Spirit, and aided to be able." The point had already been made in the controversy, that, by the Pelagian doctrine, so much power was attributed to the human will, that no one ought to pray, "Lead us not into temptation, but deliver us from evil."

If he was anxious to avoid personal controversy with Pelagius himself in the hope that he might even yet be reclaimed, Augustine was equally anxious to teach the truth on all possible occasions. Pelagius had been intimate, when at Rome, with the pious Paulinus, bishop of Nola; and it was understood that there was some tendency at Nola to follow the new teachings. It was, perhaps, as late as 414, when Augustine made reply in a long letter, to a request of Paulinus' for an exposition of certain difficult Scriptures, which had been sent him about 410. Among them was Rom. xi. 28; and, in explaining it, Augustine did not withhold a tolerably complete account of his doctrine of predestination, involving the essence of his whole teaching as to grace: "For when he had said, 'according to the election they are beloved for their father's sake,' he added, 'for the gifts and calling of God are without repentance.' You see that those are certainly meant who belong to the number of the predestinated.... 'Many indeed are called, but few chosen;' but those who are elect, these are called 'according to His purpose;' and it is beyond doubt that in them God's foreknowledge cannot be deceived. These He foreknew and predestinated to be conformed to the image of His Son, in order that He might be the first born among many brethren. But 'whom He predestinated, them He also called.' This calling is 'according to His purpose,' this calling is 'without repentance,'" etc., quoting Rom. v. 28-31. Then continuing, he says, "Those are not in this vocation, who do not persevere unto the end in the faith that worketh by love, although they walk in it a little while.... But the reason why some belong to it, and some do not, can easily be hidden, but cannot be unjust. For is there injustice with God? God forbid! For this belongs to those high judgments which, so to say, terrified the wondering apostle to look upon."

Among the most remarkable of the controversial sermons that were preached about this time, especial mention is due to two that were delivered at Carthage, midsummer of 413. The former of these was preached on the festival of John the Baptist's birth (June 24), and naturally took the forerunner for its subject. The nativity of John suggesting the nativity of Christ, the preacher spoke of the marvel of the incarnation. He who was in the beginning, and was the Word of God, and was Himself God, and who made all things, and in whom was life, even this one "came to us. To whom? To the worthy? Nay, but to the unworthy! For Christ died for the ungodly, and for the unworthy, though He was worthy. We indeed were unworthy whom He pitied; but He was worthy who pitied us, to whom we say, `For Thy pity's sake, Lord, free us!' Not for the sake of our preceding merits, but `for Thy pity's sake, Lord, free us;' and `for Thy name's sake be propitious to our sins,' not for our merit's sake.... For the merit of sins is, of course, not reward, but punishment." He then dwelt upon the necessity of the incarnation, and the necessity of a mediator between God and "the whole mass of the human race alienated from Him by Adam." Then quoting I Cor. iv. 7, he asserts that it is not our varying merits, but God's grace alone, that makes us differ, and that we are all alike, great and small, old and young, saved by one and the same Saviour. "What then, some one says," he continues, "even the infant needs a liberator? Certainly he needs one. And the witness to it is the mother that faithfully runs to church with the child to be baptized. The witness is Mother Church herself, who receives the child for washing, and either for dismissing him [from this life] freed, or nurturing him in piety.... Last of all, the tears of his own misery are witness in the child himself.... Recognize the misery, extend the help. Let all put on bowels of mercy. By as much as they cannot speak for themselves, by so much more pityingly let us speak for the little ones,"-and then follows a passage calling on the Church to take the grace of infants in their charge as orphans committed to their care, which is in substance repeated from a former sermon. The speaker proceeded to quote Matt. i. 21, and apply it. If Jesus came to save from sins, and infants are brought to Him, it is to confess that they, too, are sinners. Then, shall they be withheld from baptism? "Certainly, if the child could speak

for himself, he would repel the voice of opposition, and cry out, `Give me Christ's life! In Adam I died: give me Christ's life; in whose sight I am not clean, even if I am an infant whose life has been but one day in the earth.'
""No way can be found," adds the preacher, "of coming into the life of this world except by Adam; no way can be found of escaping punishment in the next world except by Christ. Why do you shut up the one door?" Even John the Baptist himself was born in sin; and absolutely no one can be found who was born apart from sin, until you find one who was born apart from Adam. "`By one man sin entered into the world, and by sin, death; and so it passed through upon all men.' If these were my words, could this sentiment be expressed more expressly, more clearly, more fully?"

Three days afterwards, on the invitation of the Bishop of Carthage, Augustine preached a sermon professedly directed against the Pelagians, which takes up the threads hinted at in the former discourse, and develops a full polemic with reference to the baptism of infants. He began, formally enough, with the determination of the question in dispute. The Pelagians concede that infants should be baptized. The only question is, for what are they baptized? We say that they would not otherwise have salvation and eternal life; but they say it is not for salvation, not for eternal life, but for the kingdom of God.... "The child, they say, although not baptized, by the desert of his innocence, in that he has no sin at all, either actual or original, either from him self or contracted from Adam, necessarily has salvation and eternal life even if not baptized; but is to be baptized for this reason—that he may enter into the kingdom of God, i.e., into the kingdom of heaven." He then shows that there is no eternal life outside the kingdom of heaven, no middle place between the right and left hand of the judge at the last day, and that, therefore, to exclude one from the kingdom of God is to consign him to the pains of eternal fire; while, on the other side, no one ascends into heaven unless he has been made a member of Christ, and this can only be by faith—which, in an infant's case, is professed by another in his stead. He then treats, at length, some of the puzzling questions with which the Pelagians were wont to try the catholics; and then breaking off suddenly, he took a volume in his hands. "I ask you," he said, "to bear with me a little: I will read somewhat. It is St. Cyprian whom I hold in my hand, the ancient bishop of this see. What he thought of the baptism of infants—nay, what he has shown that the

Church always thought—learn in brief. For it is not enough for them to dispute and argue, I know not what impious novelties: they even try to charge us with asserting something novel. It is on this account that I read here St. Cyprian, in order that you may perceive that the orthodox understanding and catholic sense reside in the words which I have been just now speaking to you. He was asked whether an infant ought to be baptized before he was eight days old, seeing that by the ancient law no infant was allowed to be circumcised unless he was eight days old. A question arose from this as to the day of baptism—for concerning the origin of sin there was no question; and therefore from this thing of which there was no question, that question that had arisen was settled." And then he read to them the passage out of Cyprian's letter to Fidus, which declared that he, and all the council with him, unanimously thought that infants should be baptized at the earliest possible age, lest they should die in their inherited sin, and so pass into eternal punishment. The sermon closed with a tender warning to the teachers of these strange doctrines: he might call them heretics with truth, but he will not; let the Church seek still their salvation, and not mourn them as dead; let them be exhorted as friends, not striven with as enemies. "They disparage us," he says, "we will bear it; let them not disparage the rule [of faith], let them not disparage the truth; let them not contradict the Church, which labours every day for the remission of infants' original sin. This thing is settled. The errant disputer may be borne with in other questions that have not been thoroughly canvassed, that are not yet settled by the full authority of the Church—their error should be borne with: it ought not to extend so far, that they endeavour to shake even the very foundation of the Church!" He hints that although the patience hitherto exhibited towards them is "perhaps not blameworthy," yet patience may cease to be a virtue, and become culpable negligence: in the mean time, however, he begs that the catholics should continue amicable, fraternal, placid, loving, long suffering.

Augustine himself gives us a view of the progress of the controversy at this time in a letter written in 414. The Pelagians had everywhere scattered the seeds of their new error; and although some, by his ministry and that of his brother workers, had, "by God's mercy," been cured of their pest, yet they still existed in Africa, especially about Carthage, and were everywhere propagating their opinions in subterraneous whispers, for fear of the judgment of the Church. Wherever they were not refuted, they were seducing others to their following; and they were so spread abroad that he did not know where they would break out next. Nevertheless, he was still unwilling to brand them as heretics, and was more desirous of healing them as sick members of the Church than of cutting them off finally as too diseased for cure. Jerome also tells us that the poison was spreading in both the East and the West, and mentions particularly as seats where it showed itself the islands of Rhodes and Sicily. Of Rhodes we know nothing further; but from Sicily an appeal came to Augustine in 414 from one Hilary, setting forth that there were certain Christians about Syracuse who taught strange doctrines, and beseeching Augustine to help him in dealing with them. The doctrines were enumerated as follows: "They say (1) that man can be without sin, (2) and can easily keep the commandments of God if he will; (3) that an unbaptized infant, if he is cut off by death, cannot justly perish, since he is born without sin; (4) that a rich man that remains in his riches cannot enter the kingdom of God, except he sell all that he has;... (5) that we ought not to swear at all;" (6) and, apparently, that the Church is to be in this world without spot or blemish. Augustine suspected that these Sicilian disturbances were in some way the work of Coelestius, and therefore in his answer informs his correspondent of what had been done at the Synod of Carthage (412) against him. The long letter that he sent back follows the inquiries in the order they were put by Hilary. To the first he replies, in substance, as he had treated the same matter in the second book of the treatise, On the Merits and Forgiveness of Sins, that it was opposed to Scripture, but was less a heresy than the wholly unbearable opinion that this state of sinlessness could be attained without God's help. "But when they say that free will suffices to man for fulfilling the precepts of the Lord, even though unaided to good works by God's grace and the gift of the Holy Spirit, it is to be altogether anathematized and detested with all execrations. For those who assert this are inwardly alien from God's grace, because being ignorant of God's righteousness, like the Jews of whom the apostle speaks, and wishing to establish their own, they are not subject to God's righteousness, since there is no fulfilment of the law except love; and of course the love of God is shed abroad in our hearts, not by ourselves, nor by the force of our own will, but by the Holy Ghost who is given to us." Dealing next with the second point, he drifts into the matter he had more fully developed in his work On the Spirit and the Letter . "Free will avails for God's works," he says, "if it be divinely aided, and this comes by humble seeking and doing; but when deserted by divine aid, no matter how excellent may be its knowledge of the law, it will by no means possess solidity of righteousness, but only the inflation of ungodly pride and deadly arrogance. This is taught us by that same Lord's Prayer; for it would be an empty thing for us to ask God `Lead us not into temptation,' if the matter was so placed in our power that we would avail for fulfilling it without any aid from Him. For this free will is free in proportion as it is sound, but it is sound in proportion as it is subject to divine pity and grace. For it faithfully prays, saying, `Direct my ways according to Thy word, and let no iniquity reign over me.' For how is that free over which iniquity reigns? But see who it is that is invoked by it, in order that it may not reign over it. For it says not, `Direct my ways according to free will because no iniquity shall rule over me,' but `Direct my ways according to Thy word, and let no iniquity rule over me .' It is a prayer, not a promise; it is a confession, not a profession; it is a wish for full freedom, not a boast of personal power. For it is not every one `who confides in his own power,' but `every one who calls on the name of God, that shall be saved.' `But how shall they call upon Him,' he says, `in whom they have not believed?' Accordingly, then, they who rightly believe, believe in order to call on Him in whom they have believed, and to avail for doing what they receive in the precepts of the law; since what the law commands, faith prays for." "God, therefore, commands continence, and gives continence; He commands by the law, He gives by grace; He commands by the letter, He gives by the spirit: for the law without grace makes the transgression to abound, and the letter without the spirit kills. He commands for this reason—that we who have endeavoured to do what He commands, and are worn out in our weakness under the law, may know how to ask for the aid of grace; and if we have been able to do any good work, that we may not be ungrateful to Him who aids us." The answer to the third point traverses the ground that was fully covered in the first book of the treatise On the Merits and Forgiveness of Sins , beginning by opposing the Pelagians to Paul in Rom. v. 12-19: "But when they say that an infant, cut off by death, unbaptized, cannot perish since he is born without sin—it is not this that the apostle says; and I think that it is better to believe the apostle than them." The fourth and fifth questions were new in this controversy; and it is not certain that they belong properly to it, though the legalistic asceticism of the Pelagian leaders may well have given rise to a demand on all Christians to sell what they had, and give to the poor. This one of the points, Augustine treats at length, pointing out that many of the saints of old were rich, and that the Lord and His apostles always so speak that their counsels avail to the right use, not the destruction, of wealth. Christians ought so to hold their wealth that they are not held by it, and by no means prefer it to Christ. Equal good sense and mildness are shown in his treatment of the question concerning oaths, which he points out were used by the Lord and His apostles, but advises to be used as little as possible lest by the custom of frequent oaths we learn to swear lightly. The question as to the Church, he passes over as having been sufficiently treated in the course of his previous remarks.

To the number of those who had been rescued from Pelagianism by his efforts, Augustine was now to have the pleasure of adding two others, in whom he seems to have taken much delight. Timasius and James were two young men of honorable birth and liberal education, who had, by the exhortation of Pelagius, been moved to give up the hope that they had in this world, and enter upon the service of God in an ascetic life. Naturally, they had turned to him for instruction, and had received a book to which they had given their study. They met somewhere with some of Augustine's writings, however, and were deeply affected by what he said as to grace, and now began to see that the teaching of Pelagius opposed the grace of God by which man becomes a Christian. They gave their book, therefore, to Augustine, saying that it was Pelagius', and asking him for Pelagius' sake, and for the sake of the truth, to answer it. This was done, and the resulting book, On Nature and Grace , sent to the young men, who returned a letter of thanks in which they professed their conversion from their error. In this book, too, which was written in 415, Augustine refrained from mentioning Pelagius by name, feeling it better to spare the man while not sparing his writings. But he tells us, that, on reading the book of Pelagius to which it was an answer, it became clear to him beyond any doubt that his teaching was distinctly anti-Christian; and when speaking of his own book privately to a friend, he allows himself to call it "a considerable book against the heresy of Pelagius, which he had been constrained to write by some brethren whom he had persuaded to adopt his fatal error, denying the grace of Christ." Thus his attitude towards the persons of the new teachers was becoming ever more and more strained, in despite of his full recognition of the excellent motives that might lie behind their "zeal not according to knowledge." This treatise opens with a recognition of the zeal of Pelagius, which, as it burns most ardently against those who, when reproved for sin, take refuge in censuring their nature, Augustine compares with the heathen view as expressed in Sallust's saying, "the human race falsely complains of its own nature," and which he charges with not being according to knowledge, and proposes to oppose by an equal zeal against all attempts to render the cross of Christ of none effect. He then gives a brief but excellent summary of the more important features of the catholic doctrine concerning nature and grace (2-7). Opening the work of Pelagius, which had been placed in his hands, he examines his doctrine of sin, its nature and effects. Pelagius, he points out, draws a distinction, sound enough in itself, between what is "possible" and what is "actual," but applies it unsoundly to sin, when he says that every man has the possibility of being without sin (8-9), and therefore without condemnation. Not so, says Augustine; an infant who dies unbaptized has no possibility of salvation open to him; and the man who has lived and died in a land where it was impossible for him to hear the name of Christ, has had no possibility open to him of becoming righteous by nature and free will. If this be not so, Christ is dead in vain, since all men then might have accomplished their salvation, even if Christ had never died (10). Pelagius, moreover, he shows, exhibits a tendency to deny the sinful character of all sins that are impossible to avoid, and so treats of sins of ignorance as to show that he excuses them (13-19). When he argues that no sin, because it is not a substance, can change nature, which is a substance, Augustine replies that this destroys the Saviour's work—for how can He save from sins if sins do not corrupt? And, again, if an act cannot injure a substance, how can abstention from food, which is a mere act, kill the body? In the same way sin is not a substance; but God is a substance—yea, the height of substance, and only true sustenance of the reasonable creature; and the consequence of departure from Him is to the soul what refusal of food is to the body (22). To Pelagius' assertion that sin cannot be punished by more sin, Augustine replies that the apostle thinks differently (Rom. i. 21-31). Then putting his finger on the main point in controversy, he quotes the Scriptures as declaring the present condition of man to be that of spiritual death. "The truth then designates as dead those whom this man declares to be unable to be damaged or corrupted by sin—because, forsooth, he has discovered sin to be no substance!" (25). It was by free will that man passed into this state of death; but a dead man needs something else to revive him—he needs nothing less than a Vivifier. But of vivifying grace, Pelagius knew nothing; and by knowing nothing of a Vivifier, he knows nothing of a Saviour; but rather by making nature of itself able to be sinless, he glorifies the Creator at the expense of the Saviour (39). Next is examined Pelagius' contention that many saints are enumerated in the Scriptures as having lived sinlessly in this world. While declining to discuss the question of fact as to the Virgin Mary (42), Augustine opposes to the rest the declaration of John in I John i. 8, as final, but still pauses to explain why the Scriptures do not mention the sins of all, and to contend that all who ever were saved under the Old Testament or the New, were saved by the sacrificial death of Christ, and by faith in Him (40-50). Thus we are brought, as Augustine says, to the core of the question, which concerns, not the fact of sinlessness in any man, but man's ability to be sinless. This ability Pelagius affirms of all men, and Augustine denies of all "unless they are justified by the grace of God through our Lord Jesus Christ and Him crucified" (51). Thus, the whole discussion is about grace, which Pelagius does not admit in any true sense, but places only in the nature that God has made (52). We are next invited to attend to another distinction of Pelagius', in which he discriminates sharply between the nature that God has made, the crown of which is free will, and the use that man makes of this free will. The endowment of free will is a "capacity;" it is, because given by God in our making, a necessity of nature, and not in man's power to have or not have. It is the right use of it only, which man has in his power. This analysis, Pelagius illustrates at length, by appealing to the difference between the possession and use of the various bodily senses. The ability to see, for instance, he says, is a necessity of our nature; we do not make it, we cannot help having it; it is ours only to use it. Augustine criticises this presentation of the matter with great sharpness (although he is not averse to the analysis itself)—showing the inapplicability of the illustrations used— for, he asks, is it not possible for us to blind ourselves, and so no longer have the ability to see? and would not many a man like to control the "use" of his "capacity" to hear when a screechy saw is in the neighbourhood? (55); and as well the falsity of the contention illustrated, since Pelagius has ignored the fall, and, even were that not so, has so ignored the need of God's aid for all good, in any state of being, as to deny it (56). Moreover, it is altogether a fallacy, Augustine argues, to contend that men have the "ability" to make every use we can conceive of our faculties. We cannot wish for unhappiness; God cannot deny Himself (57); and just so, in a corrupt nature, the mere possession of a faculty of choice does not imply the ability to use that faculty for not sinning. "Of a man, indeed, who has his legs strong and sound, it may be said admissibly enough, 'whether he will or not, he has the capacity of walking;' but if his legs be broken, however much he may wish, he has not the `capacity.' The nature of which our author speaks is corrupted" (57). What, then, can he mean by saying that, whether we will or not, we have the capacity of not sinning—a statement so opposite to Paul's in Rom. vii. 15? Some space is next given to an attempted rebuttal by Pelagius of the testimony of Gal. v. 17, on the ground that the "flesh" there does not refer to the baptized (60-70); and then the passages are examined which Pelagius had quoted against Augustine out of earlier writers—Lactantius (71), Hilary (72), Ambrose (75), John of Constantinople (76), Xystus—a blunder of Pelagius, who quoted from a Pythagorean philosopher, mistaking him for the Roman bishop Sixtus (57), Jerome (78), and Augustine himself (80). All these writers, Augustine shows, admitted the universal sinfulness of man—and especially he himself had confessed the necessity of grace in the immediate context of the passage quoted by Pelagius. The treatise closes (82 sq.) with a noble panegyric on that love which God sheds abroad in the heart, by the Holy Ghost, and by which alone we can be made keepers of the law.

    The treatise On Nature and Grace was as yet unfinished, when the over-busy scriptorium at Hippo was invaded by another young man seeking instruction. This time it was a zealous young presbyter from the remotest part of Spain, "from the shore of the ocean,"—Paulus Orosius by name, whose pious soul had been afflicted with grievous wounds by the Priscillianist and Origenist heresies that had broken out in his country, and who had come with eager haste to Augustine, on hearing that he could get from him the instruction which he needed for confuting them. Augustine seems to have given him his heart at once; and, feeling too little informed as to the special heresies which he wished to be prepared to controvert, persuaded him to go on to Palestine to be taught by Jerome, and gave him introductions which described him as one "who is in the bond of catholic peace a brother, in point of age a son, and in honour a fellow-presbyter—a man of quick understanding, ready speech, and burning zeal." His departure to Palestine gave Augustine an opportunity to consult with Jerome on the one point that had been raised in the Pelagian controversy on which he had not been able to see light. The Pelagians had early argued, that, if souls are created anew for men at their birth, it would be unjust in God to impute Adam's sin to them. And Augustine found himself unable either to prove that souls are transmitted (traduced, as the phrase is), or to show that it would not involve God in injustice to make a soul only to make it subject to a sin committed by another. Jerome had already put himself on record as a believer in both original sin and the creation of souls at the time of birth. Augustine feared the logical consequences of this assertion, and yet was unable to refute it. He therefore seized this occasion to send a long treatise on the origin of the soul to his friend, with the request that he would consider the subject anew, and answer his doubts. In this treatise he stated that he was fully persuaded that the soul had fallen into sin, but by no fault of God or of nature, but of its own free will; and asked when could the soul of an infant have contracted the guilt, which, unless the grace of Christ should come to its rescue by baptism, would involve it in condemnation, if God (as Jerome held, and as he was willing to hold with him, if this difficulty could be cleared up) makes each soul for each individual at the time of birth? He professed himself embarrassed on such a supposition by the penal sufferings of infants, the pains they endured in this life, and much more the danger they are in of eternal damnation, into which they actually go unless saved by baptism. God is good, just, omnipotent: how, then, can we account for the fact that "in Adam all die," if souls are created afresh for each birth? "If new souls are made for men," he affirms, "individually at their birth, I do not see, on the one hand, that they could have any sin while yet in infancy; nor do I believe, on the other hand, that God condemns any soul which He sees to have no sin;" "and yet, whoever says that those children who depart out of this life without partaking of the sacrament of baptism, shall be made alive in Christ, certainly contradicts the apostolic declaration," and "he that is not made alive in Christ must necessarily remain under the condemnation of which the apostle says that by the offence of one, judgment came upon all men to condemnation." "Wherefore," he adds to his correspondent, "if that opinion of yours does not contradict this firmly grounded article of faith, let it be mine also; but if it does, let it no longer be yours." So far as obtaining light was concerned, Augustine might have spared himself the pain of this composition: Jerome simply answered that he had no leisure to reply to the questions submitted to him. But Orosius' mission to Palestine was big with consequences. Once there, he became the accuser of Pelagius before John of Jerusalem, and the occasion, at least, of the trials of Pelagius in Palestine during the summer and winter of 415 which issued so disastrously, and ushered in a new phase of the conflict.

Meanwhile, however, Augustine was ignorant of what was going on in the East, and had his mind directed again to Sicily. About a year had passed since he had sent thither his long letter to Hilary. Now his conjecture that Coelestius was in some way at the bottom of the Sicilian outbreak, received confirmation from a paper which certain catholic brethren brought out of Sicily, and which was handed to Augustine by two exiled Spanish bishops, Eutropius and Paul. This paper bore the title, Definitions Ascribed to Coelestius, and presented internal evidence, in style and thought, of being correctly so ascribed. It consisted of three parts, in the first of which were collected a series of brief and compressed "definitions," or "ratiocinations" as Augustine calls them, in which the author tries to place the catholics in a logical dilemma, and to force them to admit that man can live in this world without sin. In the second part, he adduced certain passages of Scripture in defence of his doctrine. In the third part, he undertook to deal with the texts that had been quoted against his contention, not, however, by examining into their meaning, or seeking to explain them in the sense of his theory, but simply by matching them with others which he thought made for him. Augustine at once (about the end of 415) wrote a treatise in answer to this, which bears the title of On the Perfection of Man's Righteousness. The distribution of the matter in this work follows that of the treatise to which it is an answer. First of all (1-16), the "ratiocinations" are taken up one by one and briefly answered. As they all concern sin, and have for their object to prove that man cannot be accounted a sinner unless he is able, in his own power, wholly to avoid sin—that is, to prove that a plenary natural ability is the necessary basis of responsibility—Augustine argues per contra that man can entail a sinfulness on himself for which and for the deeds of which he remains responsible, though he is no longer able to avoid sin; thus admitting that for the race, plenary ability must stand at the root of sinfulness. Next (17-22) he discusses the passages which Coelestius had advanced in defence of his teachings, viz., (1) passages in which God commands men to be without sin, which Augustine meets by saying that the point is, whether these commands are to be fulfilled without God's aid, in the body of this death, while absent from the Lord (17-20); and (2) passages in which God declares that His commandments are not grievous, which Augustine meets by explaining that all God's commandments are fulfilled only by Love, which finds nothing grievous; and that this love is shed abroad in our hearts by the Holy Ghost, without whom we have only fear, to which the commandments are not only grievous, but impossible. Lastly, Augustine patiently follows Coelestius through his odd "oppositions of texts," explaining carefully all that he had adduced, in an orthodox sense (23-42). In closing, he takes up Coelestius' statement, that "it is quite possible for man not to sin even in word, if God so will," pointing out how he avoids saying "if God give him His help," and then proceeds to distinguish carefully between the differing assertions of sinlessness that may be made. To say that any man ever lived, or will live, without needing forgiveness, is to contradict Rom. v. 12, and must imply that he does not need a Saviour, against Matt. ix. 12, 13. To say that after his sins have been forgiven, any one has ever remained without sin, contradicts I John i. 8 and Matt. vi. 12. Yet, if God's help be allowed, this contention is not so wicked as the other; and the great heresy is to deny the necessity of God's constant grace, for which we pray when we say, "Lead us not into temptation."

Tidings were now (416) beginning to reach Africa of what was doing in the East. There was diligently circulated everywhere, and came into Augustine's hands, an epistle of Pelagius' own "filled with vanity," in which he boasted that fourteen bishops had approved his assertion that "man can live without sin, and easily keep the commandments if he wishes," and had thus "shut the mouth of opposition in confusion," and "broken up the whole band of wicked conspirators against him." Soon afterwards a copy of an "apologetical paper," in which Pelagius used the authority of the Palestinian bishops against his adversaries, not altogether without disingenuousness, was sent by him to Augustine through the hands of a common acquaintance, Charus by name. It was not accompanied, however, by any letter from Pelagius; and Augustine wisely refrained from making public use of it. Towards midsummer Orosius came with more authentic information, and bearing letters from Jerome and Heros and Lazarus. It was apparently before his coming that a controversial sermon was preached, only a fragment of which has come down to us. So far as we can learn from the extant part, its subject seems to have been the relation of prayer to Pelagianism; and what we have, opens with a striking anecdote: "When these two petitions-'Forgive us our debts as we also forgive our debtors,' and `Lead us not into temptation'-are objected to the Pelagians, what do you think they reply? I was horrified, my brethren, when I heard it. I did not, indeed, hear it with my own ears; but my holy brother and fellow-bishop Urbanus, who used to be presbyter here, and now is bishop of Sicca," when he was in Rome, and was arguing with one who held these opinions, pressed him with the weight of the Lord's Prayer, and "what do you think he replied to him? `We ask God,' he said, `not to lead us into temptation, lest we should suffer something that is not in our power— lest I should be thrown from my horse; lest I should break my leg; lest a robber should slay me, and the like. For these things,' he said, `are not in my power; but for overcoming the temptations of my sins, I both have ability if I wish to use it, and am not able to receive God's help.' You see, brethren," the good bishop adds, "how malignant this heresy is: you see how it horrifies all of you. Have a care that you be not taken by it." He then presses the general doctrine of prayer as proving that all good things come from God, whose aid is always necessary to us, and is always attainable by prayer; and closes as follows: "Consider, then, these things, my brethren, when any one comes to you and says to you, `What, then, are we to do if we have nothing in our power, unless God gives all things? God will not then crown us, but He will crown Himself.' You already see that this comes from that vein: it is a vein, but it has poison in it; it is stricken by the serpent; it is not sound. For what Satan is doing to-day is seeking to cast out from the Church by the poison of heretics, just as he once cast out from Paradise by the poison of the serpent. Let no one tell you that this one was acquitted by the bishops: there was an acquittal, but it was his confession, so to speak, his amendment, that was acquitted. For what he said before the bishops seemed catholic; but what he wrote in his books, the bishops who pronounced the acquittal were ignorant of. And perchance he was really convinced and amended. For we ought not to despair of the man who perchance preferred to be united to the catholic faith, and fled to its grace and aid. Perchance this was what happened. But, in any event, it was not the heresy that was acquitted, but the man who denied the heresy."

The coming of Orosius must have dispelled any lingering hope that the meaning of the council's finding was that Pelagius had really recanted. Councils were immediately assembled at Carthage and Mileve, and the documents which Orosius had brought were read before them. We know nothing of their proceedings except what we can gather from the letters which they sent to Innocent at Rome, seeking his aid in their condemnation of the heresy now so nearly approved in Palestine. To these two official letters, Augustine, in company with four other bishops, added a third private letter, in which they took care that Innocent should be informed on all the points necessary to his decision. This important letter begins almost abruptly with a characterization of Pelagianism as inimical to the grace of God, and has grace for its subject throughout. It accounts for the action of the Palestinian synod, as growing out of a misunderstanding of Pelagius' words, in which he seemed to acknowledge grace, which these catholic bishops understood naturally to mean that grace of which they read in the Scriptures, and which they were accustomed to preach to their people—the grace by which we are justified from iniquity, and saved from weakness; while he meant nothing more than that by which we are given free will at our creation. "For if these bishops had understood that he meant only that grace which we have in common with the ungodly and with all, along with whom we are men, while he denied that by which we are Christians and the sons of God, they not only could not have patiently listened to him—they could not even have borne him before their eyes." The letter then proceeds to point out the difference between grace and natural gifts, and between grace and the law, and to trace out Pelagius' meaning when he speaks of grace, and when he contends that man can be sinless without any really inward aid. It suggests that Pelagius be sent for, and thoroughly examined by Innocent, or that he should be examined by letter or in his writings; and that he be not cleared until he unequivocally confessed the grace of God in the catholic sense, and anathematized the false teachings in the books attributed to him. The book of Pelagius which was answered in the treatise On Nature and Grace was enclosed, with this letter, with the most important passages marked: and it was suggested that more was involved in the matter than the fate of one single man, Pelagius, who, perhaps, was already brought to a better mind; the fate of multitudes already led astray, or yet to be deceived by these false views, was in danger.

At about this same time (417), the tireless bishop sent a short letter to a Hilary, who seems to be Hilary of Norbonne, which is interesting from its undertaking to convey a characterization of Pelagianism to one who was as yet ignorant of it. It thus brings out what Augustine conceived to be its essential features. "An effort has been made," we read, "to raise a certain new heresy, inimical to the grace of Christ, against the Church of Christ. It is not yet openly separated from the Church. It is the heresy of men who dare to attribute so much power to human weakness that they contend that this only belongs to God's grace—that we are created with free will and the possibility of not sinning, and that we receive God's commandments which are to be fulfilled by us; but, for keeping and fulfilling these commandments, we do not need any divine aid. No doubt, the remission of sins is necessary for us; for we have no power to right what we have done wrong in the past. But for avoiding and overcoming sins in the future, for conquering all temptations with virtue, the human will is sufficient by its natural capacity without any aid of God's grace. And neither do infants need the grace of the Saviour, so as to be liberated by it through His baptism from perdition, seeing that they have contracted no contagion of damnation from Adam." He engages Hilary in the destruction of this heresy, which ought to be "concordantly condemned and anathematized by all who have hope in Christ," as a "pestiferous impiety," and excuses himself for not undertaking its full refutation in a brief letter. A much more important letter was sent off, at about the same time, to John of Jerusalem, who had conducted the first Palestinian examination of Pelagius, and had borne a prominent part in the synod at Diospolis. He sent with it a copy of Pelagius' book which he had examined in his treatise On Nature and Grace , as well as a copy of that reply itself, and asked John to send him an authentic copy of the proceedings at Diospolis. He took this occasion seriously to warn his brother bishop against the wiles of Pelagius, and begged him, if he loved Pelagius, to let men see that he did not so love him as to be deceived by him. He pointed out that in the book sent with the letter, Pelagius called nothing the grace of God except nature; and that he affirmed, and even vehemently contended, that by free will alone, human nature was able to suffice for itself for working righteousness and keeping all God's commandments; whence any one could see that he opposed the grace of God of which the apostles spoke in Rom. vii. 24, 25, and contradicted, as well, all the prayers and benedictions of the Church by which blessings were sought for men from God's grace. "If you love Pelagius, then," he continued, "let him, too, love you as himself—nay, more than himself; and let him not deceive you. For when you hear him confess the grace of God and the aid of God, you think he means what you mean by it. But let him be openly asked whether he desires that we should pray God that we sin not; whether he proclaims the assisting grace of God, without which we would do much evil; whether he believes that even children who have not yet been able to do good or evil are nevertheless, on account of one man by whom sin entered into the world, sinners in him, and in need of being delivered by the grace of Christ." If he openly denies such things, Augustine would be pleased to hear of it.

Thus we see the great bishop sitting in his library at Hippo, placing his hands on the two ends of the world. That nothing may be lacking to the picture of his universal activity, we have another letter from him, coming from about this same time, that exhibits his care for the individuals who had placed themselves in some sort under his tutelage. Among the refugees from Rome in the terrible times when Alaric was a second time threatening the city, was a family of noble women—Proba, Juliana, and Demetrias, -grandmother, mother, and daughter—who, finding an asylum in Africa, gave themselves to God's service, and sought the friendship and counsel of Augustine. In 413 the granddaughter "took the veil" under circumstances that thrilled the Christian world, and brought out letters of congratulation and advice from Augustine and Jerome, and also from Pelagius. This letter of Pelagius seems not to have fallen into Augustine's way until now (416): he was so disturbed by it that he wrote to Juliana a long letter warning her against its evil counsels. It was so shrewdly phrased, that, at first sight, Augustine was himself almost persuaded that it did somehow acknowledge the grace of God; but when he compared it with others of Pelagius' writings, he saw that here, too, he was using ambiguous phrases in a non-natural sense. The object of his letter (in which Alypius is conjoined, as joint author) to Juliana is to warn her and her holy daughter against all opinions that opposed the grace of God, and especially against the covert teaching of the letter of Pelagius to Demetrias.

"In this book," he says, "were it lawful for such an one to read it, a virgin of Christ would read that her holiness and all her spiritual riches are to spring from no other source than herself; and thus before she attains to the perfection of blessedness, she would learn-which may God forbid!-to be ungrateful to God." Then, after quoting the words of Pelagius, in which he declares that "earthly riches came from others, but your spiritual riches no one can have conferred on you but yourself; for these, then, you are justly praised, for these you are deservedly to be preferred to others—for they can exist only from yourself and in yourself," he continues: "Far be it from any virgin to listen to statements like these. Every virgin of Christ understands the innate poverty of the human heart, and therefore declines to be adorned otherwise than by the gifts of her spouse.... Let her not listen to him who says, `No one can confer them on you but yourself, and they cannot exist except from you and in you:' but to him who says, `We have this treasure in earthen vessels, that the excellency of the power may be of God, and not of us.' And be not surprised that we speak of these things as yours, and not from you; for we speak of daily bread as `ours,' but yet add `give it to us,' lest it should be thought it was from ourselves." Again, he warns her that grace is not mere knowledge any more than mere nature; and that Pelagius, even when using the word "grace," means no inward or efficient aid, but mere nature or knowledge or forgiveness of past sins; and beseeches her not to forget the God of all grace from whom (Wisdom i. 20, 21) Demetrias had that very virgin continence which was so justly her boast.

With the opening of 417, came the answers from Innocent to the African letters. And although they were marred by much boastful language concerning the dignity of his see, which could not but be distasteful to the Africans, they admirably served their purpose in the satisfactory manner in which they, on the one hand, asserted the necessity of the "daily grace, and help of God," for our good living, and, on the other, determined that the Pelagians had denied this grace, and declared their leaders Pelagius and Coelestius deprived of the communion of the Church until they should "recover their senses from the wiles of the Devil by whom they are held captive according to his will." Augustine may be pardoned for supposing that a condemnation pronounced by two provincial synods in Africa, and heartily concurred in by the Roman bishop, who had already at Jerusalem been recognized as in some sort the fit arbiter of this Western dispute, should settle the matter. If Pelagius had been before jubilant, Augustine found this a suitable time for his rejoicing.

About the same time with Innocent's letters, the official proceedings of the synod of Diospolis at last reached Africa, and Augustine lost no time (early in 417) in publishing a full account and examination of them, thus providing us with that inestimable boon, a full contemporary history of the chief events connected with the controversy up to this time. This treatise, which is addressed to Aurelius, bishop of Carthage, opens with a brief explanation of Augustine's delay heretofore, in discussing Pelagius' defence of himself in Palestine, as due to his not having received the official copy of the Proceedings of the Council at Diospolis (1-2 a). Then Augustine proceeds at once to discuss at length the doings of the synod, point by point, following the official record step by step (2 b -45). He treats at large here eleven items in the indictment, with Pelagius' answers and the synod's decision, showing that in all of them Pelagius either explained away his heresy, taking advantage of the ignorance of the judges of his books, or else openly repudiated or anathematized it. When the twelfth item of the indictment was reached (41 b -43), Augustine shows that the synod was so indignant at its character (it charged Pelagius with teaching that men cannot be sons of God unless they are sinless, and with condoning sins of ignorance, and with asserting that choice is not free if it depends on God's help, and that pardon is given according to merit), that, without waiting for Pelagius' answer, it condemned the statement, and Pelagius at once repudiated and anathematized it (43). How could the synod act in such circumstances, he asks, except by acquitting the man who condemned the heresy? After quoting the final judgment of the synod (44), Augustine briefly characterizes it and its effect (45) as being indeed all that could be asked of the judges, but of no moral weight to those better acquainted than they were with Pelagius' character and writings. In a word, they approved his answers to them, as indeed they ought to have done; but they by no means approved, but both they and he condemned, his heresies as expressed in his writings. To this statement, Augustine appends an account of the origin of Pelagianism, and of his relations to it from the beginning, which has the very highest value as history (46-49); and then speaks of the character and doubtful practices of Pelagius (50-58), returning at the end (59-65) to a thorough canvass of the value of the acquittal which he obtained by such doubtful practices at the synod. He closes with an indignant account of the outrages which the Pelagians had perpetrated on Jerome (66).

This valuable treatise is not, however, the only account of the historical origin of Pelagianism that we have, from Augustine's hands. Soon after the death of Innocent (March 12, 417), he found occasion to write a very long letter to the venerable Paulinus of Nola, in which he summarized both the history of and the arguments against this "worldly philosophy." He begins by saying that he knows Paulinus has loved Pelagius as a servant of God, but is ignorant in what way he now loves him. For he himself not only has loved him, but loves him still, but in different ways. Once he loved him as apparently a brother in the true faith: now he loves him in the longing that God will by His mercy free him from his noxious opinions against God's grace. He is not merely following report in so speaking of him: no doubt report did for a long time represent this of him, but he gave the less heed to it because report is accustomed to lie. But a book of his at last came into his hands, which left no room for doubt, since in it he asserted repeatedly that God's grace consisted of the gift to man of the capacity to will and act, and thus reduced it to what is common to pagans and Christians, to the ungodly and godly, to the faithful and infidels. He then gives a brief account of the measures that had been taken against Pelagius, and passes on to a treatment of the main matters involved in the controversy—all of which gather around the one magic word of "the grace of God." He argues first that we are all lost—in one mass and concretion of perdition—and that God's grace alone makes us to differ. It is therefore folly to talk of deserving the beginnings of grace. Nor can a faithful man say that he merits justification by his faith, although it is given to faith; for at once he hears the words, "what hast thou that thou didst not receive?" and learns that even the deserving faith is the gift of God. But if, peering into God's inscrutable judgments, we go farther, and ask why, from the mass of Adam, all of which undoubtedly has fallen from one into condemnation, this vessel is made for honor, that for dishonor—we can only say that we do not know more than the fact; and God's reasons are hidden, but His acts are just. Certain it is that Paul teaches that all die in Adam; and that God freely chooses, by a sovereign election, some out of that sinful mass, to eternal life; and that He knew from the beginning to whom He would give this grace, and so the number of the saints has always been fixed, to whom he gives in due time the Holy

Ghost. Others, no doubt, are called; but no others are elect, or "called according to his purpose." On no other body of doctrines, can it be possibly explained that some infants die unbaptized, and are lost. Is God unjust to punish innocent children with eternal pains? And are they not innocent if they are not partakers of Adam's sin? And can they be saved from that, save by the undeserved, and that is the gratuitous, grace of God? The account of the Proceedings at the Palestinian synod is then taken up, and Pelagius' position in his latest writings is quoted and examined. "But why say more?" he adds.... "Ought they not, since they call themselves Christians, to be more careful than the Jews that they do not stumble at the stone of offence, while they subtly defend nature and free will just like philosophers of this world who vehemently strive to be thought, or to think themselves, to attain for themselves a happy life by the force of their own will? Let them take care, then, that they do not make the cross of Christ of none effect by the wisdom of word (I Cor. i. 17), and thus stumble at the rock of offence. For human nature, even if it had remained in that integrity in which it was created, could by no means have served its own Creator without His aid. Since then, without God's grace it could not keep the safety it had received, how can it without God's grace repair what it has lost?" With this profound view of the Divine immanence, and of the necessity of His moving grace in all the acts of all his creatures, as over against the heathen-deistic view of Pelagius, Augustine touched in reality the deepest point in the whole controversy, and illustrated the essential harmony of all truth.

The sharpest period of the whole conflict was now drawing on. Innocent's death brought Zosimus to the chair of the Roman See, and the efforts which he made to re-instate Pelagius and Coelestius now began (September, 417). How little the Africans were likely to yield to his remarkable demands, may be seen from a sermon which Augustine preached on the 23d of September, while Zosimus' letter (written on the 21st of September) was on its way to Africa. The preacher took his text from John vi. 54-66. "We hear here," he said, "the true Master, the Divine Redeemer, the human Saviour, commending to us our ransom, His blood. He calls His body food, and His blood drink; and, in commending such food and drink, He says, `Unless you eat My flesh, and drink My blood, ye shall have no life in you.' What, then, is this eating and drinking, but to live? Eat life, drink life; you shall have life, and life is whole. This will come—that is, the body and blood of Christ will be life to every one—if what is taken visibly in the sacrament is in real truth spiritually eaten and spiritually drunk. But that He might teach us that even to believe in Him is of gift, not of merit, He said, `No one comes to Me, except the Father who sent Me draw him.' Draw him, not lead him. This violence is done to the heart, not the flesh. Why do you marvel? Believe, and you come; love, and you are drawn. Think not that this is harsh and injurious violence; it is soft, it is sweet; it is sweetness itself that draws you. Is not the sheep drawn when the succulent herbage is shown to him? And I think that there is no compulsion of the body, but an assembling of the desire. So, too, do you come to Christ; wish not to plan a long journey—when you believe, then you come. For to Him who is everywhere, one comes by loving, not by taking a voyage. No doubt, if you come not, it is your work; but if you come, it is God's work. And even after you have come, and are walking in the right way, become not proud, lest you perish from it: `happy are those that confide in Him,' not in themselves, but in Him. We are saved by grace, not of ourselves: it is the gift of God. Why do I continually say this to you? It is because there are men who are ungrateful to grace, and attribute much to unaided and wounded nature. It is true that man received great powers of free will at his creation; but he lost them by sinning. He has fallen into death; he has been made weak; he has been left half dead in the way, by robbers; the good Samaritan has lifted him up upon his ass, and borne him to the inn. Why should we boast? But I am told that it is enough that sins are remitted in baptism. But does the removal of sin take away weakness too? What! will you not see that after pouring the oil and the wine into the wounds of the man left half dead by the robbers, he must still go to the inn where his weakness may be healed? Nay, so long as we are in this life we bear a fragile body; it is only after we are redeemed from corruption that we shall find no sin, and receive the crown of righteousness. Grace, that was hidden in the Old Testament, is now manifest to the whole world. Even though the Jew may be ignorant of it, why should Christians be enemies of grace? why presumptuous of themselves? why ungrateful to grace? For, why did Christ come? Was not nature already here—that very nature by the praise of which you are beguiled? Was not the law here? But the apostle says, `If righteousness is of the law, then is Christ dead in vain.' What the apostle says of the law, that we say to these men about nature: if righteousness is by nature, then Christ is dead in vain. What then was said of the Jews, this we see repeated in these men. They have a zeal for God: I bear them witness that they have a zeal for God, but not according to knowledge. For, being ignorant of God's righteousness, and wishing to establish their own, they are not subject to the righteousness of God. My brethren, share my compassion. Where you find such men, wish no concealment; let there be no perverse pity in you: where you find them, wish no concealment at all. Contradict and refute, resist, or persuade them to us. For already two councils have, in this cause, sent letters to the Apostolic See, whence also rescripts have come back. The cause is ended: would that the error might some day end! Therefore we admonish so that they may take notice, we teach so that they may be instructed, we pray so that their way be changed." Here is certainly tenderness to the persons of the teachers of error; readiness to forgive, and readiness to go all proper lengths in recovering them to the truth. But here is also absolute firmness as to the truth itself, and a manifesto as to policy. Certainly, on the lines of the policy here indicated, the Africans fought out the coming campaign. They met in council at the end of this year, or early in the next (418); and formally replied to Zosimus, that the cause had been tried, and was finished, and that the sentence that had been already pronounced against Pelagius and Coelestius should remain in force until they should unequivocally acknowledge that "we are aided by the grace of God through Christ, not only to know, but to do, what is right, and that in each single act; so that without grace we are unable to have, think, speak, or do anything belonging to piety." As we may see Augustine's hand in this, so, doubtless, we may recognize it in that remarkable piece of engineering which crushed Zosimus' plans within the next few months. There is, indeed, no direct proof that it was due to Augustine, or to the Africans under his leading, or to the Africans at all, that the State interfered in the matter; it is even in doubt whether the action of the Empire was put forth as a rescript, or as a self-moved decree: but surely it is difficult to believe that such a coup de thÈ,tre could have been prepared for Zosimus by chance; and as it is well known, both that Augustine believed in the righteousness of civil penalty for heresy, and invoked it on other occasions, and defended and used it on this, and that he had influential friends at court with whom he was in correspondence, it seems, on internal grounds, altogether probable that he was the Deus ex machin, who let loose the thunders of ecclesiastical and civil enactment simultaneously on the poor Pope's devoted head.

The "great African Council" met at Carthage, on the 1st of May, 418; and, after its decrees were issued, Augustine remained at Carthage, and watched the effect of the combination of which he was probably one of the moving causes. He had now an opportunity to betake himself once more to his pen. While still at Carthage, at short notice, and in the midst of much distraction, he wrote a large work, in two books which have come down to us under the separate titles of On the Grace of Christ, and On Original Sin, at the instance of another of those ascetic families which formed so marked a feature in those troubled times. Pinianus and Melania, the daughter of Albina, were husband and wife, who, leaving Rome amid the wars with Alaric, had lived in continence in Africa for some time, but now in Palestine had separated, he to become head of a monastery, and she an inmate of a convent. While in Africa, they had lived at Sagaste under the tutelage of Alypius, and in the enjoyment of the friendship and instruction of Augustine. After retiring to Bethlehem, like the other holy ascetics whom he had known in Africa, they kept up their relations with him. Like the others, also, they became acquainted with Pelagius in Palestine, and were well-nigh deceived by him. They wrote to Augustine that they had begged Pelagius to condemn in writing all that had been alleged against him, and that he had replied in the presence of them all, that "he anathematized the man who either thinks or says that the grace of God whereby Christ Jesus came into the world to save sinners is not necessary, not only for every hour and for every moment, but also for every act of our lives," and asserted that "those who endeavor to disannul it are worthy of everlasting punishment." Moreover, they wrote that Pelagius had read to them, out of his book that he had sent to Rome, his assertion "that infants ought to be baptized with the same formula of sacramental words as adults." They wrote that they were delighted to hear these words from Pelagius, as they seemed exactly what they had been desirous of hearing; and yet they preferred consulting Augustine about them, before they were fully committed regarding them. It was in answer to this appeal, that the present work was written; the two books of which take up the two points in Pelagius' asseveration—the theme of the first being "the assistance of the Divine grace towards our justification, by which God co-operates in all things for good to those who love

Him, and whom He first loved, giving to them that He may receive from them,"-while the subject of the second is "the sin which by one man has entered the world along with death, and so has passed upon all men."

The first book, On the Grace of Christ, begins by quoting and examining Pelagius' anathema of all those who deny that grace is necessary for every action (2 sq.). Augustine confesses that this would deceive all who were not fortified by knowledge of Pelagius' writings; but asserts that in the light of them it is clear that he means that grace is always necessary, because we need continually to remember the forgiveness of our sins, the example of Christ, the teaching of the law, and the like. Then he enters (4 sq.) upon an examination of Pelagius' scheme of human faculties, and quotes at length his account of them given in his book, In Defence of Free Will, wherein he distinguishes between the possibilitas (posse), voluntas (velle), and actio (esse), and declares that the first only is from God and receives aid from God, while the others are entirely ours, and in our own power. Augustine opposes to this the passage in Phil. ii. 12, 13 (6), and then criticises (7 sq.) Pelagius' ambiguous acknowledgment that God is to be praised for man's good works, "because the capacity for any action on man's part is from God," by which he reduces all grace to the primeval endowment of nature with "capacity" (possibilitas, posse), and the help afforded it by the law and teaching. Augustine points out the difference between law and grace, and the purpose of the former as a pedagogue to the latter (9 sq.), and then refutes Pelagius' further definition of grace as consisting in the promise of future glory and the revelation of wisdom, by an appeal to Paul's thorn in the flesh, and his experience under its discipline (11 sq.). Pelagius' illustrations from our senses, of his theory of natural faculty, are then sharply tested (16) ; and the criticism on the whole doctrine is then made and pressed (17 sq.), that it makes God equally sharer in our blame for evil acts as in our praise for good ones, since if God does help, and His help is only His gift to us of ability to act in either part, then He has equally helped to the evil deeds as to the good. The assertion that this "capacity of either part" is the fecund root of both good and evil is then criticised (19 sq.), and opposed to Matt. vii. i8, with the result of establishing that we must seek two roots in our dispositions for so diverse results—covetousness for evil, and love for good—not a single root for both in nature. Man's "capacity," it is argued, is the root of nothing; but it is capable of both good and evil according to the moving cause, which, in the case of evil, is man-originated, while, in the case of good, it is from God (21). Next, Pelagius' assertion that grace is given according to our merits (23 sq.) is taken up and examined. It is shown, that, despite his anathema, Pelagius holds to this doctrine, and in so extreme a form as explicitly to declare that man comes and cleaves to God by his freedom of will alone, and without God's aid. He shows that the Scriptures teach just the opposite (24-26); and then points out how Pelagius has confounded the functions of knowledge and love (27 sq.), and how he forgets that we cannot have merits until we love God, while John certainly asserts that God loved us first (I John iv. 10). The representation that what grace does is to render obedience easier (28-30), and the twin view that prayer is only relatively necessary, are next criticised (32). That Pelagius never acknowledges real grace, is then demonstrated by a detailed examination of all that he had written on the subject (31-45). The book closes (46-80) with a full refutation of Pelagius' appeal to Ambrose, as if he supported him; and exhibition of Ambrose's contrary testimony as to grace and its necessity.

The object of the second book- On Original Sin -is to show, that, in spite of Pelagius' admissions as to the baptism of infants, he yet denies that they inherit original sin and contends that they are born free from corruption. The book opens by pointing out that there is no question as to Coelestius' teaching in this matter (2-8), as he at Carthage refused to condemn those who say that Adam's sin injured no one but himself, and that infants are born in the same state that Adam was in before the fall, and openly asserted at Rome that there is no sin ex traduce . As for Pelagius, he is simply more cautious and mendacious than Coelestius: he deceived the Council at Diospolis, but failed to deceive the Romans (5-13), and, as a matter of fact (14-18), teaches exactly what Coelestius does. In support of this assertion, Pelagius' Defence of Free Will is quoted, wherein he asserts that we are born neither good nor bad, "but with a capacity for either," and "as without virtue, so without vice; and previous to the action of our own proper will, that that alone is in man which God has formed" (14). Augustine also quotes Pelagius' explanation of his anathema against those who say Adam's sin injured only himself, as meaning that he has injured man by setting a bad "example," and his even more sinuous explanation of his anathema against those who assert that infants are born in the same condition that Adam was in before he fell, as meaning that they are infants and he was a man! (16-18). With this introduction to them, Augustine next treats of Pelagius' subterfuges (19-25), and then animadverts on the importance of the issue (26-37), pointing out that Pelagianism is not a mere error, but a deadly heresy, and strikes at the very centre of Christianity. A counter argument of the Pelagians is then answered (38-45), "Does not the doctrine of original sin make marriage an evil thing?" No, says Augustine, marriage is ordained by God, and is good; but it is a diseased good, and hence what is born of it is a good nature made by God, but this good nature in a diseased condition—the result of the Devil's work. Hence; if it be asked why God's gift produces any thing for the Devil to take possession of, it is to be answered that God gives his gifts liberally (Matt. v. 45), and makes men; but the Devil makes these men sinners (46). Finally, as Ambrose had been appealed to in the former book, so at the end of this it is shown that he openly proclaimed the doctrine of original sin, and here too, before Pelagius, condemned Pelagius (47 sq.).

What Augustine means by writing to Pinianus and his family that he was more oppressed by work at Carthage than anywhere else, may perhaps be illustrated from his diligence in preaching while in that capital. He seems to have been almost constantly in the pulpit, during this period "of the sharpest conflict with them," preaching against the Pelagians. There is one series of his sermons, of the exact dates of which we can be pretty sure, which may be adverted to here—Sermons 151 and 152, preached early in October, 418; Sermon 155 on Oct. 14, 156 on Oct.17, and 26 on Oct. 18; thus following one another almost with the regularity of the days. The first of these was based on Rom. vii. 15-25, which he declares to contain dangerous words if not properly understood; for men are prone to sin, and when they hear the apostle so speaking they do evil, and think they are like him. They are meant to teach us, however, that the life of the just in this body is a war, not yet a triumph: the triumph will come only when death is swallowed up in victory. It would, no doubt, be better not to have an enemy than even to conquer. It would be better not to have evil desires: but we have them; therefore, let us not go after them. If they rebel against us, let us rebel against them; if they fight, let us fight; if they besiege, let us besiege: let us look only to this, that they do not conquer. With some evil desires we are born: others we make, by bad habit. It is on account of those with which we are born, that infants are baptized; that they may be freed from the guilt of inheritance, not from any evil of custom, which, of course, they have not. And it is on account of these, too, that our war must be endless: the concupiscence with which we are born cannot be done away as long as we live; it may be diminished, but not done away. Neither can the law free us, for it only reveals the sin to our greater apprehension. Where, then, is hope, save in the superabundance of grace? The next sermon (152) takes up the words in Rom. viii. 1-4, and points out that the inward aid of the Spirit brings all the help we need. "We, like farmers in the field, work from without: but, if there were no one who worked from within, the seed would not take root in the ground, nor would the sprout arise in the field, nor would the shoot grow strong and become a tree, nor would branches and fruit and leaves be produced. Therefore the apostle distinguishes between the work of the workmen and of the Creator (I Cor. iii. 6, 7). If God give not the increase, empty is this sound within your ears; but if he gives, it avails somewhat that we plant and water, and our labor is not in vain." He then applies this to the individual, striving against his lusts; warns against Manichean error; and distinguishes between the three laws—the law of sin, the law of faith, and the law of deeds—defending the latter, the law of Moses, against the Manicheans; and then he comes to the words of the text, and explains its chief phrases, closing thus: "What other do we read here than that Christ is a sacrifice for sin? ...Behold by what `sin' he condemned sin: by the sacrifice which he made for sins, he condemned sin. This is the law of the Spirit of life which has freed you from the law of sin and death. For that other law, the law of the letter, the law that commands, is indeed good; `the commandment is holy and just and good:' but `it was weak by the flesh,' and what it commanded it could not bring about in us. Therefore there is one law, as I began by saying, that reveals sin to you, and another that takes it away: the law of the letter reveals sin, the law of grace takes it away." Sermon 155 covers the same ground, and more, taking the broader text, Rom. viii. 1-11, and fully developing its teaching, especially as discriminating between the law of sin and the law of Moses and the law of faith; the law of Moses being the holy law of God written with His finger on the tables of stone, while the law of the Spirit of life is nothing other than the same law written in the heart, as the prophet (Jer. xxx. 1, 33) clearly declares. So written, it does not terrify from without, but soothes from within. Great care is also taken, lest by such phrases as, "walk in the Spirit, not in the flesh," "who shall deliver me from the body of this death?" a hatred of the body should be begotten. "Thus you shall be freed from the body of this death, not by having no body, but by having another one and dying no more. If, indeed, he had not added, 'of this death,' perchance an error might have been suggested to the human mind, and it might have been said, 'You see that God does not wish us to have a body.' But He says, 'the body of this death.' Take away death, and the body is good. Let our last enemy, death, be taken away, and my dear flesh will be mine for eternity. For no one can ever 'hate his own flesh.' Although the 'spirit lusts against the flesh, and the flesh against the spirit,' although there is now a battle in this house, yet the husband is seeking by his strife not the ruin of, but concord with, his wife. Far be it, far be it, my brethren, that the spirit should hate the flesh in lusting against it! It hates the vices of the flesh; it hates the wisdom of the flesh; it hates the contention of death. This corruption shall put on incorruption—this mortal shall put on immortality; it is sown a natural body; it shall rise a spiritual body; and you shall see full and perfect concord—you shall see the creature praise the Creator." One of the special interests of such passages is to show, that, even at this early date, Augustine was careful to guard his hearers from Manichean error while proclaiming original sin. One of the sermons which, probably, was preached about this time (153), is even entitled, "Against the Manicheans openly, but tacitly against the Pelagians," and bears witness to the early development of the method that he was somewhat later to use effectively against Julian's charges of Manicheanism against the catholics. Three days afterwards, Augustine preached on the next few verses, Rom. viii. 12-17, but can scarcely be said to have risen to the height of its great argument. The greater part of the sermon is occupied with a discussion of the law, why it was given, how it is legitimately used, and its usefulness as a pedagogue to bring us to Christ; then of the need of a mediator; and then, of what it is to live according to the flesh, which includes living according to merely human nature; and the need of mortifying the flesh in this world. All this, of course, gave full opportunity for opposing the leading Pelagian errors; and the sermon is brought to a close by a direct polemic against their assertion that the function of grace is only to make it more easy to do what is right. "With the sail more easily, with the oar with more difficulty: nevertheless even with the oar we can go. On a beast more easily, on foot with more difficulty: nevertheless progress can be made on foot. It is not true! For the true Master who flatters no one, who deceives no one—the truthful Teacher and very Saviour to whom the most grievous pedagogue has led us—when he was speaking about good works, i.e., about the fruits of the twigs and branches, did not say, 'Without me, indeed, you can do something, but you will do it more easily with me;' He did not say, 'You can make your fruit without me, but more richly with me.' He did not say this! Read what He said: it is the holy gospel—bow the proud necks! Augustine does not say this: the Lord says it. What says the Lord? 'Without me you can do nothing!' " "On the very next day, he was again in the pulpit, and taking for his text chiefly the ninety-fourth Psalm. The preacher began by quoting the sixth verse, and laying stress on the words "our Maker." 'No Christian,' he said, 'doubted that God had made him, and that in such a sense that God created not only the first man, from whom all have descended, but that God to-day creates every man—as He said to one of His saints, "Before that I formed thee in the womb, I knew thee." At first He created man apart from man; now He creates man from man: nevertheless, whether man apart from man, or man from man, "it is He that made us, and not we ourselves." Nor has He made us and then deserted us; He has not cared to make us, and not cared to keep us. Will He who made us without being asked, desert us when He is besought? But is it not just as foolish to say, as some say or are ready to say, that God made them men, but they make themselves righteous? Why, then, do we pray to God to make us righteous? The first man was created in a nature that was without fault or flaw. He was made righteous: he did not make himself righteous; what he did for himself was to fall and break his righteousness. This God did not do: He permitted it, as if He had said, "Let him desert Me; let him find himself; and let his misery prove that he has no ability without Me." In this way God wished to show man what free will was worth without God. O evil free will without God! Behold, man was made good; and by free will man was made evil! When will the evil man make himself good by free will? When good, he was not able to keep himself good; and now that he is evil, is he to make himself good? Nay, behold, He that made us has also made us "His people" (Ps. xciv. 7). This is a distinguishing gift. Nature is common to all, but grace is not. It is not to be confounded with nature; but if it were, it would still be gratuitous. For certainly no man, before he existed, deserved to come into existence. And yet

God has made him, and that not like the beasts or a stock or a stone, but in His own image. Who has given this benefit? He gave it who was in existence: he received it who was not. And only He could do this, who calls the things that are not as though they were: of whom the apostle says that "He chose us before the foundation of the world." We have been made in this world, and yet the world was not when we were chosen. Ineffable! wonderful! They are chosen who are not: neither does He err in choosing, nor choose in vain. He chooses, and has elect whom He is to create to be chosen: He has them in Himself; not indeed in His nature, but in His prescience. Let us not, then, glory in ourselves, or dispute against grace. If we are men, He made us. If we are believers, He made us this too. He who sent the Lamb to be slain has, out of wolves, made us sheep. This is grace. And it is an even greater grace than that grace of nature by which we were all made men.' "I am continually endeavouring to discuss such things as these," said the preacher, "against a new heresy which is attempting to rise; because I wish you to be fixed in the good, untouched by the evil....For, disputing against grace in favor of free will, they became an offence to pious and catholic ears. They began to create horror; they began to be avoided as a fixed pest; it began to be said of them, that they argued against grace. And they found such a device as this:`Because I defend man's free will, and say that free will is sufficient in order that I may be righteous,' says one, `I do not say that it is without the grace of God.' The ears of the pious are pricked up, and he who hears this, already begins to rejoice: `Thanks be to God! He does not defend free will without the grace of God! There is free will, but it avails nothing without the grace of God' If, then, they do not defend free will without the grace of God, what evil do they say? Expound to us, O teacher, what grace you mean? `When I say,' he says, `the free will of man, you observe that I say " of man "?' What then? `Who created man?' God. `Who gave him free will?' God. `If, then, God created man, and God gave man free will, whatever man is able to do by free will, to whose grace does he owe it, except to His who made him with free will?' And this is what they think they say so acutely! You see, nevertheless, my brethren, how they preach that general grace by which we were created and by which we are men; and, of course, we are men in common with the ungodly, and are Christians apart from them. It is this grace by which we are Christians, that we wish them to preach, this that we wish them to acknowledge, this that we wish—of which the apostle says, 'I do not make void the grace of God, for if righteousness is by the law, Christ is dead in vain.' "Then the true function of the law is explained, as a revealer of our sinfulness, and a pedagogue to lead us to Christ: the Manichean view of the Old Testament law is attacked, but its insufficiency for salvation is pointed out; and so we are brought back to the necessity of grace, which is illustrated from the story of the raising of the dead child in 2 Kings iv. 18-37—the dead child being Adam; the ineffective staff (by which we ought to walk), the law; but the living prophet, Christ with his grace, which we must preach. "The prophetic staff was not enough for the dead boy: would dead nature itself have been enough? Even this, by which we are made, although we nowhere read of it under this name, we nevertheless, because it is given gratuitously, confess to be grace. But we show to you a greater grace than this, by which we are Christians.... This is the grace by Jesus Christ our Lord: it was He that made us—both before we were at all, it was He that made us, and now, after we are made, it is He that has made us all righteous—and not we ourselves." There was but one mass of perdition from Adam, to which nothing was due but punishment; and from that mass vessels have been made unto honor. "Rejoice because you have escaped; you have escaped the death that was due—you have received the life that was not due. 'But,' you ask, 'why did He make me unto honor, and another unto dishonor?' Will you who will not hear the apostle saying, 'O man, who art thou that repliest against God?' hear Augustine?... Do you wish to dispute with me? Nay, wonder with me, and cry out with me, 'Oh the depth of the riches!' Let us both be afraid—let us both cry out, 'Oh the depth of the riches!' Let us both agree in fear, lest we perish in error."

Augustine was not less busy with his pen, during these months, than with his voice. Quite a series of letters belong to the last half of 418, in which he argues to his distant correspondents on the same themes which he was so iterantly trying to make clear to his Carthaginian auditors. One of the most interesting of these was written to a fellow-bishop, Optatus, on the origin of the soul. Optatus, like Jerome, had expressed himself as favoring the theory of a special creation of each at birth; and Augustine, in this letter as in the paper sent to Jerome, lays great stress on so holding our theories on so obscure a matter as to conform to the indubitable fact of the transmission of sin. This fact, such passages as I Cor. xv. 21 sq., Rom. v. 12 sq., make certain; and in stating this, Augustine takes the opportunity to outline the chief contents of the catholic faith over against the Pelagian denial of original sin and grace: that all are born under the contagion of death and in the bond of guilt; that there is no deliverance except in the one Mediator, Christ Jesus; that before His coming men received him as promised, now as already come, but with the same faith; that the law was not intended to save, but to shut up under sin and so force us back upon the one Saviour; and that the distribution of grace is sovereign. Augustine pries into God's sovereign counsels somewhat more freely here than is usual with him. "But why those also are created who, the Creator foreknew, would belong to damnation, not to grace, the blessed apostle mentions with as much succinct brevity as great authority. For he says that God, 'wishing to show His wrath and demonstrate His power,' etc. (Rom. ix. 22). Justly, however, would he seem unjust in forming vessels of wrath for perdition, if the whole mass from Adam were not condemned. That, therefore, they are made on birth vessels of anger, belongs to the punishment due to them; but that they are made by re-birth vessels of mercy, belongs to the grace that is not due to them. God, therefore, shows his wrath—not, of course, perturbation of mind, such as is called wrath among men, but a just and fixed vengeance.... He shows also his power, by which he makes a good use of evil men, and endows them with many natural and temporal goods, and bends their evil to admonition and instruction of the good by comparison with it, so that these may learn from them to give thanks to God that they have been made to differ from them, not by their own deserts which were of like kind in the same mass, but by His pity.... But by creating so many to be born who, He foreknew, would not belong to his grace, so that they are more by an incomparable multitude than those whom he deigned to predestinate as children of the promise into the glory of His Kingdom—He wished to show by this very multitude of the rejected how entirely of no moment it is to the just God what is the multitude of those most justly condemned. And that hence also those who are redeemed from this condemnation may understand, that what they see rendered to so great a part of the mass was the due of the whole of it—not only of those who add many others to original sin, by the choice of an evil will, but as well of so many children who are snatched from this life without the grace of the Mediator, bound by no bond except that of original sin alone." With respect to the question more immediately concerning which the letter was written, Augustine explains that he is willing to accept the opinion that souls are created for men as they are born, if only it can be made plain that it is consistent with the original sin that the Scriptures so clearly teach. In the paper sent to Jerome, the difficulties of creationism are sufficiently urged; this letter is interesting on account of its statement of some of the difficulties of traducianism also—thus evidencing Augustine's clear view of the peculiar complexity of the problem, and justifying his attitude of balance and uncertainty between the two theories. 'The human understanding,' he says, 'can scarcely comprehend how a soul arises from a parent's soul in the offspring; or is transmitted to the offspring as a candle is lighted from a candle and thence another fire comes into existence without loss to the former one. Is there an incorporeal seed for the soul, which passes, by some hidden and invisible channel of its own, from the father to the mother, when it is conceived in the woman? Or, even more incredible, does it lie enfolded and hidden within the corporeal seed?' He is lost in wonder over the question whether, when conception does not take place, the immortal seed of an immortal soul perishes; or, does the immortality attach itself to it only when it lives? He even expresses the doubt whether traducianism will explain what it is called in to explain, much better than creationism; in any case, who denies that God is the maker of every soul? Isaiah (lvii. 16) says, "I have made every breath;" and the only question that can arise is as to method—whether He "makes every breath from the one first breath, just as He makes every body of man from the one first body; or whether he makes new bodies indeed, from the one body, but new souls out of nothing." Certainly nothing but Scripture can determine such a question; but where do the Scriptures speak unambiguously upon it? The passages to which the creationists point only affirm the admitted fact that God makes the soul; and the traducianists forget that the word "soul" in the Scriptures is ambiguous, and can mean "man," and even a "dead man." What more can be done, then, than to assert what is certain, viz., that sin is propagated, and leave what is uncertain in the doubt in which God has chosen to place it?

    This letter was written not long after the issue of Zosimus' Tractoria, demanding the signature of all to African orthodoxy; and Augustine sends Optatus "copies of the recent letters which have been sent forth from the Roman see, whether specially to the African bishops or generally to all bishops," on the Pelagian controversy, "lest perchance they had not yet reached" his correspondent, who, it is very evident, he was anxious should thoroughly realize "that the authors, or certainly the most energetic and noted teachers," of these new heresies, "had been condemned in the whole Christian world by the vigilance of episcopal councils aided by the Saviour who keeps His Church, as well as by two venerable overseers of the Apostolical see, Pope Innocent and Pope Zosimus, unless they should show repentance by being convinced and reformed." To this zeal we owe it that the letter contains an extract from Zosimus' Tractoria, one of the two brief fragments of that document that have reached our day.

There was another ecclesiastic in Rome, besides Zosimus, who was strongly suspected of favoring the Pelagians—the presbyter Sixtus, who afterwards became Pope Sixtus III. But when Zosimus sent forth his condemnation of Pelagianism, Sixtus sent also a short letter to Africa addressed to Aurelius of Carthage, which, though brief, indicated a considerable vigor against the heresy which he was commonly believed to have before defended, and which claimed him as its own. Some months afterwards, he sent another similar, but longer, letter to Augustine and Alypius, more fully expounding his rejection of "the fatal dogma" of Pelagius, and his acceptance of "that grace of God freely given by Him to small and great, to which Pelagius' dogma was diametrically opposed." Augustine was overjoyed with these developments. He quickly replied in a short letter in which he expresses the delight he has in learning from Sixtus' own hand that he is not a defender of Pelagius, but a preacher of grace. And close upon the heels of this he sent another much longer letter, in which he discusses the subtler arguments of the Pelagians with an anxious care that seems to bear witness to his desire to confirm and support his correspondent in his new opinions. Both letters testify to Augustine's approval of the persecuting measures which had been instituted by the Roman see in obedience to the emperor; and urge on Sixtus his duty not only to bring the open heretics to deserved punishment, but to track out those who spread their poison secretly, and even to remember those whom he had formerly heard announcing the error before it had been condemned, and who were now silent through fear, and to bring them either to open recantation of their former beliefs, or to punishment. It is pleasanter to recall our thoughts to the dialectic of these letters. The greater part of the second is given to a discussion of the gratuitousness of grace, which, just because grace, is given to no preceding merits. Many subtle objections to this doctrine were brought forward by the Pelagians. They said that "free will was taken away if we asserted that man did not have even a good will without the aid of God;" that we made "God an accepter of persons, if we believed that without any preceding merits He had mercy on whom He would, and whom He would He called, and whom He would He made religious;" that "it was unjust, in one and the same case, to deliver one and punish another;" that, if such a doctrine is preached, "men who do not wish to live rightly and faithfully, will excuse themselves by saying that they have done nothing evil by living ill, since they have not received the grace by which they might live well;" that it is a puzzle "how sin can pass over to the children of the faithful, when it has been remitted to the parents in baptism;" that "children respond truly by the mouth of their sponsors that they believe in remission of sins, but not because sins are remitted to them , but because they believe that sins are remitted in the church or in baptism to those in whom they are found, not to those in whom they do not exist," and consequently they said that "they were unwilling that infants should be so baptized unto remission of sins as if this remission took place in them," for (they contend) "they have no sin ; but they are to be baptized, although without sin, with the same rite of baptism through which remission of sins takes place in any that are sinners." This last objection is especially interesting because it furnishes us with the reply which the Pelagians made to the argument that Augustine so strongly pressed against them from the very act and ritual of baptism, as implying remission of sins. His rejoinder to it here is to point to the other parts of the same ritual, and to ask why, then, infants are exorcised and exsufflated in baptism. "For, it cannot be doubted that this is done fictitiously, if the Devil does not rule over them; but if he rules over them, and they are therefore not falsely exorcised and exsufflated, why does that prince of sinners rule over them except because of sin?" On the fundamental matter of the gratuitousness of grace, this letter is very explicit. "If we seek for the deserving of hardening, we shall find it.... But if we seek for the deserving of pity, we shall not find it; for there is none, lest grace be made a vanity if it is not given gratis, but rendered to merits. But, should we say that faith preceded and in it there is desert of grace, what desert did man have before faith that he should receive faith? For, what did he have that he did not receive? and if he received it, why does he glory as if he received it not? For as man would not have wisdom, understanding, prudence, fortitude, knowledge, piety, fear of God, unless he had received (according to the prophet) the spirit of wisdom and understanding, of prudence and fortitude, of knowledge and piety and the fear of God ; as he would not have justice, love, continence, except the spirit was received of whom the apostle says, `For you did not receive the spirit of fear, but of virtue, and love, and continence:' so he would not have faith unless he received the spirit of faith of whom the same apostle says, `Having then the same spirit of faith, according to what is written, "I believed and therefore spoke," we too believe and therefore speak.' But that He is not received by desert, but by His mercy who has mercy on whom He will, is manifestly shown where he says of himself, `I have obtained mercy to be faithful.' ""If we should say that the merit of prayer precedes, that the gift of grace may follow,...even prayer itself is found among the gifts of grace" (Rom. viii. 26). "It remains, then, that faith itself, whence all righteousness takes beginning;...it remains, I say, that even faith itself is not to be attributed to the human will which they extol, nor to any preceding merits, since from it begin whatever good things are merits: but it is to be confessed to be the gratuitous gift of God, since we consider it true grace, that is, without merits, inasmuch as we read in the same epistle, `God divides out the measure of faith to each' (Rom. xii. 3). Now, good works are done by man, but faith is wrought in man, and without it these are not done by any man. For all that is not of faith is sin" (Rom. xiv. 23.

By the same messenger who carried this important letter to Sixtus, Augustine sent also a letter to Mercator, an African layman who was then apparently at Rome, but who was afterwards (in 429) to render service by instructing the Emperor Theodosius as to the nature and history of Pelagianism, and so preventing the appeal of the Pelagians to him from being granted. Now he appears as an inquirer: Augustine, while at Carthage, had received a letter from him in which he had consulted him on certain questions that the Pelagians had raised, but in such a manner as to indicate his opposition to them. Press of business had compelled the postponement of the reply until this later date. One of the questions that Mercator had put concerned the Pelagian account of infants sharing in the one baptism unto remission of sins, which we have seen Augustine answering when writing to Sixtus. In this letter he replies: "Let them, then, hear the Lord (John iii. 36). Infants, therefore, who made believers by others, by whom they are brought to baptism, are, of course, unbelievers by others, if they are in the hands of such as do not believe that they should be brought, inasmuch as they believe they are nothing profited; and accordingly, if they believe by believers, and have eternal life, they are unbelievers by unbelievers, and shall not see life, but the wrath of God abideth on them. For it is not said, 'it comes on them,' but 'it abideth on them,' because it was on them from the beginning, and will not be taken from them except by the grace of God through Jesus Christ, our Lord....Therefore, when children are baptized, the confession is made that they are believers, and it is not to be doubted that those who are not believers are condemned: let them, then, dare to say now, if they can, that they contract no evil from their origin to be condemned by the just God, and have no contagion of sin." The other matter on which Mercator sought light concerned the statement that universal death proved universal sin: he reported that the Pelagians replied that not even death was universal—that Enoch, for instance, and Elijah, had not died. Augustine adds those who are to be found living at the second advent, who are not to die, but be "changed;" and replies that Rom. v. 12 is perfectly explicit that there is no death in the world except that which comes from sin, and that God a Saviour, and we cannot at all "deny that He is able to do that, now, in any that he wishes, without death, which we undoubtingly believe is to be done in so many after death." He adds that the difficult question is not why Enoch and Elijah did not die, if death is the punishment of sin; but why, such being the case, the justified ever die; and he refers his correspondent to his book On the Baptism of Infants for a resolution of this greater difficulty.

It was probably at the very end of 418 that Augustine wrote a letter of some length to Asellicus, in reply to one which he had written on "avoiding the deception of Judaism," to the primate of the Bizacene province, and which that ecclesiastic had sent to Augustine for answering. He discusses in this the law of the Old Testament. He opens by pointing out that the apostle forbids Christians to Judaize (Gal. ii. 14-16), and explains that it is not merely the ceremonial law that we may not depend upon, "but also what is said in the law, 'Thou shalt not covet' (which no one, of course, doubts is to be said to Christians too), does not justify man, except by faith in Jesus Christ and the grace of God through Jesus Christ our Lord." He then expounds the use of the law: "This, then, is the usefulness of the law: that it shows man to himself, so that he may know his weakness, and see how, by the prohibition, carnal concupiscence is rather increased than healed....The use of the law is, thus, to convince man of his weakness, and force him to implore the medicine of grace that is in Christ." "Since these things are so," he adds, "those who rejoice that they are Israelites after the flesh, and glory in the law apart from the grace of Christ, these are those concerning whom the apostle said that `being ignorant of God's righteousness, and wishing to establish their own, they are not subject to God's righteousness;' since he calls `God's righteousness' that which is from God to man; and `their own,' what they think that the commandments suffice for them to do without the help and gift of Him who gave the law. But they are like those who, while they profess to be Christians, so oppose the grace of Christ, that they suppose that they fulfil the divine commands by human powers, and, `wishing to establish their own,' are `not subject to the righteousness of God,' and so, not indeed in name, but yet in error, Judaize. This sort of men found heads for themselves in Pelagius and Coelestius, the most acute asserters of this impiety, who by God's recent judgment, through his diligent and faithful servants, have been deprived even of catholic communion, and, on account of an impenitent heart, persist still in their condemnation."

At the beginning of 419, a considerable work was published by Augustine on one of the more remote corollaries which the Pelagians drew from his teachings. It had come to his ears, that they asserted that his doctrine condemned marriage: "if only sinful offspring come from marriage," they asked, "is not marriage itself made a sinful thing?" The book which Augustine composed in answer to this query, he dedicated to, and sent along with an explanatory letter to, the Comes Valerius, a trusted servant of the Emperor Honorius, and one of the most steady opponents at court of the Pelagian heresy. Augustine explains why he has desired to address the book to him: first, because Valerius was a striking example of those continent husbands of which that age furnishes us with many instances, and, therefore, the discussion would have especial interest for him; secondly, because of his eminence as an opponent of Pelagianism; and, thirdly, because Augustine had learned that he had read a Pelagian document in which Augustine was charged with condemning marriage by defending original sin. The book in question is the first book of the treatise On Marriage and Concupiscence . It is, naturally, tinged, or rather stained, with the prevalent ascetic notions of the day. Its doctrine is that marriage is good, and God is the maker of the offspring that comes from it, although now there can be no begetting and hence no birth without sin. Sin made concupiscence, and now concupiscence perpetuates sinners. The specific object of the work, as it states it itself, is "to distinguish between the evil of carnal concupiscence, from which man, who is born therefrom, contracts original sin, and the good of marriage" (I. 1). After a brief introduction, in which he explains why he writes, and why he addresses his book to Valerius (1-2), Augustine points out that conjugal chastity, like its higher sister-grace of continence, is God's gift. Thus copulation, but only for the propagation of children, has divine allowance (3-5). Lust, or "shameful concupiscence," however, he teaches, is not of the essence, but only an accident, of marriage. It did not exist in Eden, although true marriage existed there; but arose from, and therefore only after, sin (6-7). Its addition to marriage does not destroy the good of marriage: it only conditions the character of the offspring (8). Hence it is that the apostle allows marriage, but forbids the "disease of desire" (1 Thess. iv. 3-5); and hence the Old-Testament saints were even permitted more than one wife, because, by multiplying wives, it was not lust, but offspring, that was increased (9-10). Nevertheless, fecundity is not to be thought the only good of marriage: true marriage can exist without offspring, and even without cohabitation (11-13), and cohabitation is now, under the New Testament, no longer a duty as it was under the Old Testament (14-15), but the apostle praises continence above it. We must, then, distinguish between the goods of marriage, and seek the best (16-19). But thus it follows that it is not due to any inherent and necessary evil in marriage, but only to the presence, now, of concupiscence in all cohabitation, that children are born under sin, even the children of the regenerate, just as from the seed of olives only oleasters grow (20-24). And yet again, concupiscence is not itself sin in the regenerate; it is remitted as guilt in baptism: but it is the daughter of sin, and it is the mother of sin, and in the unregenerate it is itself sin, as to yield to it is even to the regenerate (25-39). Finally, as so often, the testimony of Ambrose is appealed to, and it is shown that he too teaches that all born from cohabitation are born guilty (40). In this book, Augustine certainly seems to teach that the bond of connection by which Adam's sin is conveyed to his offspring is not mere descent, or heredity, or mere inclusion in him, in a realistic sense, as partakers of the same numerical nature, but concupiscence. Without concupiscence in the act of generation, the offspring would not be a partaker of Adam's sin. This he had taught also previously, as, e.g., in the treatise On Original Sin, from which a few words may be profitably quoted as succinctly summing up the teaching of this book on the subject: "It is, then, manifest, that that must not be laid to the account of marriage, in the absence of which even marriage would still have existed....Such, however, is the present condition of mortal men, that the connubial intercourse and lust are at the same time in action....Hence it follows that infants, although incapable of sinning, are yet not born without the contagion of sin,...not, indeed, because of what is lawful, but on account of that which is unseemly: for, from what is lawful, nature is born; from what is unseemly, sin" (42).

Towards the end of the same year (419), Augustine was led to take up again the vexed question of the origin of the soul—both in a new letter to Optatus, by the zeal of the same monk, Renatus, who had formerly brought Optatus' inquiries to his notice—in an elaborate treatise entitled On the Soul and its Origin, by way of reply to a rash adventure of a young man named Vincentius Victor, who blamed him for his uncertainty on such a subject, and attempted to determine all the puzzles of the question, though, as Augustine insists, on assumptions that were partly Pelagian and partly worse. Optatus had written in the hope that Augustine had heard by this time from Jerome, in reply to the treatise he had sent him on this subject. Augustine, in answering his letter, expresses his sorrow that he has not yet been worthy of an answer from Jerome, although five years had passed away since he wrote, but his continued hope that such an answer will in due time come. For himself, he confesses that he has not yet been able to see how the soul can contract sin from Adam and yet not itself be contracted from Adam; and he regrets that Optatus, although holding that God creates each soul for its birth, has not sent him the proofs on which he depends for that opinion, nor met its obvious difficulties. He rebukes Optatus for confounding the question of whether God makes the soul, with the entirely different one of how he makes it, whether ex propagine or sive propagine. No one doubts that God makes the soul, as no one doubts that He makes the body. But when we consider how he makes it, sobriety and vigilance become necessary lest we should unguardedly fall into the Pelagian heresy. Augustine defends his attitude of uncertainty, and enumerates the points as to which he has no doubt: viz., that the soul is spirit, not body; that it is rational or intellectual; that it is not of the nature of God, but is so far a mortal creature that it is capable of deterioration and of alienation from the life of God, and so far immortal that after this life it lives on in bliss or punishment forever; that it was not incarnated because of, or according to, preceding deserts acquired in a previous existence, yet that it is under the curse of sin which it derives from Adam, and therefore in all cases alike needs redemption in Christ.

The whole subject of the nature and origin of the soul, however, is most fully discussed in the four books which are gathered together under the common title of On the Soul and its Origin. Vincentius Victor was a young layman who had recently been converted from the Rogatian heresy; on being shown by his friend Peter, a presbyter, a small work of Augustine's on the origin of the soul, he expressed surprise that so great a man could profess ignorance on a matter so intimate to his very being, and, receiving encouragement, wrote a book for Peter in which he attacked and tried to solve all the difficulties of the subject. Peter received the work with transports of delighted admiration; but Renatus, happening that way, looked upon it with distrust, and, finding that Augustine was spoken of in it with scant courtesy, felt it his duty to send him a copy of it, which he did in the summer of 419. It was probably not until late in the following autumn that Augustine found time to take up the matter; but then he wrote to Renatus, to Peter, and two books to Victor himself, and it is these four books together which constitute the treatise that has come down to us. The first book is a letter to Renatus, and is introduced by an expression of thanks to him for sending Victor's book, and of kindly feeling towards and appreciation for the high qualities of Victor himself (1-3). Then Victor's errors are pointed out—as to the nature of the soul (4-9), including certain far-reaching corollaries that flow from these (10-15), as well as, as to the origin of the soul(16-30); and the letter closes with some remarks on the danger of arguing from the silence of Scripture (31), on the self-contradictions of Victor (34), and on the errors that must be avoided in any theory of the origin of the soul that hopes to be acceptable—to wit, that souls become sinful by an alien original sin, that unbaptized infants need no salvation, that souls sinned in a previous state, and that they are condemned for sins which they have not committed but would have committed had they lived longer. The second book is a letter to Peter, warning him of the responsibility that rests on him as Victor's trusted friend and a clergyman, to correct Victor's errors, and reproving him for the uninstructed delight he had taken in Victor's crudities. It opens by asking Peter what was the occasion of the great joy which Victor's book brought him? could it be that he learned from it, for the first time, the old and primary truths it contained? (2-3); or was it due to the new errors that it proclaimed—seven of which he enumerates? (4-16). Then, after animadverting on the dilemma in which Victor stood, of either being forced to withdraw his violent assertion of creationism, or else of making God unjust in His dealings with new souls (17), he speaks of Victor's unjustifiable dogmatism in the matter (18-21), and closes with severely solemn words to Peter on his responsibility in the premises (22-23). In the third and fourth books, which are addressed to Victor, the polemic, of course, reaches its height. The third book is entirely taken up with pointing out to Victor, as a father to a son, the errors into which he has fallen, and which, in accordance with his professions of readiness for amendment, he ought to correct. Eleven are enumerated: 1. That the soul was made by God out of Himself (3-7); 2. That God will continuously create souls forever (8); 3. That the soul has desert of good before birth (9); 4. (contradictingly), That the soul has desert of evil before birth (10); 5. That the soul deserved to be sinful before any sin (11); 6. That unbaptized infants are saved (12); 7. That what God predestinates may not occur (13) ; 8. That Wisd. iv. 1 is spoken of infants (14); 9. That some of the mansions with the Father are outside of God's kingdom (15-17); 10. That the sacrifice of Christ's blood may be offered for the unbaptized (18); 11. That the unbaptized may attain at the resurrection even to the kingdom of heaven (19). The book closes by reminding Victor of his professions of readiness to correct his errors, and warning him against the obstinacy that makes the heretic (20-23). The fourth book deals with the more personal elements of the controversy, and discusses the points in which Victor had expressed dissent from Augustine. It opens with a statement of the two grounds of complaint that Victor had urged against Augustine; viz., that he refused to express a confident opinion as to the origin of the soul, and that he affirmed that the soul was not corporeal, but spirit (1-2). These two complaints are then taken up at length (2-16 and 17-37). To the first, Augustine replies that man's knowledge is at best limited, and often most limited about the things nearest to him; we do not know the constitution of our bodies; and, above most others, this subject of the origin of the soul is one on which no one but God is a competent witness. Who remembers his birth? Who remembers what was before birth? But this is just one of the subjects on which God has not spoken unambiguously in the Scriptures. Would it not be better, then, for Victor to imitate Augustine's cautious ignorance, than that Augustine should imitate Victor's rash assertion of errors? That the soul is not corporeal, Augustine argues (18-35) from the Scriptures and from the phenomena of dreams; and then shows, in opposition to Victor's trichotomy, that the Scriptures teach the identity of "soul" and "spirit" (36-37). The book closes with a renewed enumeration of Victor's eleven errors (38), and a final admonition to his rashness (39). It is pleasant to know that Augustine found in this case, also, that righteousness is the fruit of the faithful wounds of a friend. Victor accepted the rebuke, and professed his better instruction at the hands of his modest but resistless antagonist.

The controversy now entered upon a new stage. Among the evicted bishops of Italy who refused to sign Zosimus' Epistola Tractoria, Julian of Eclanum was easily the first, and at this point he appears as the champion of Pelagianism. It was a sad fate that arrayed this beloved son of his old friend against Augustine, just when there seemed to be reason to hope that the controversy was at an end, and the victory won, and the plaudits of the world were greeting him as the saviour of the Church. But the now fast-aging bishop was to find, that, in this "very confident young man," he had yet to meet the most persistent and most dangerous advocate of the new doctrines that had arisen. Julian had sent, at an earlier period, two letters to Zosimus, one of which has come down to us as a "Confession of Faith," and the other of which attempted to approach Augustineian forms of speech as much as possible; the object of both being to gain standing ground in the Church for the Italian Pelagians. Now he appears as a Pelagian controversialist; and in opposition to the book On Marriage and Concupiscence, which Augustine had sent Valerius, he published an extended work in four thick books addressed to Turbantius. Extracts from the first of these books were sent by some one to Valerius, and were placed by him in the hands of Alypius, who was then in Italy, for transmission to Augustine. Meanwhile, a letter had been sent to Rome by Julian, designed to strengthen the cause of Pelagianism there; and a similar one, in the names of the eighteen Pelagianizing Italian bishops, was addressed to Rufus, bishop of Thessalonica, and representative of the Roman see in that portion of the Eastern Empire which was regarded as ecclesiastically a part of the West, the design of which was to obtain the powerful support of this important magnate, perhaps, also, a refuge from persecution within his jurisdiction. These two letters came into the bands of the new Pope, Boniface, who gave them also to Alypius for transmission to Augustine. Thus provided, Alypius returned to Africa. The tactics of all these writings of Julian were essentially the same; he attempted not so much to defend Pelagianism, as to attack Augustineianism, and thus literally to carry the war into Africa. He insisted that the corruption of nature which Augustine taught was nothing else than Manicheism; that the sovereignty of grace, as taught by him, was only the attribution of "acceptance of persons," and partiality, to God; and that his doctrine of predestination was mere fatalism. He accused the anti-Pelagians of denying the goodness of the nature that God had created, of the marriage that He had ordained, of the law that He had given, of the free will that He had implanted in man, as well as the perfection of His saints. He insisted that this teaching also did dishonour to baptism itself which it professed so to honour, inasmuch as it asserted the continuance of concupiscence after baptism—and thus taught that baptism does not take away sins, but only shaves them off as one shaves his beard, and leaves the roots whence the sins may grow anew, and need cutting down again. He complained bitterly of the way in which Pelagianism had been condemned—that bishops had been compelled to sign a definition of dogma, not in council assembled, but sitting at home; and he demanded a rehearing of the whole case before a lawful council, lest the doctrine of the Manichees should be forced upon the acceptance of the world.

Augustine felt a strong desire to see the whole work of Julian against his book On Marriage and Concupiscence before he undertook a reply to the excerpts sent him by Valerius; but he did not feel justified in delaying obedience to that officer's request, and so wrote at once two treatises, one an answer to these excerpts, for the benefit of Valerius, constituting the second book of his On Marriage and Concupiscence ; and the other, a far more elaborate examination of the letters sent by Boniface, which bears the title, Against Two Letters of the Pelagians . The purpose of the second book of On Marriage and Concupiscence , Augustine himself states, in its introductory sentences, to be "to reply to the taunts of his adversaries with all the truthfulness and scriptural authority he could command." He begins (2) by identifying the source of the extracts forwarded to him by Valerius, with Julian's work against his first book, and then remarks upon the garbled form in which he is quoted in them (3-6), and passes on to state and refute Julian's charge that the catholics had turned Manicheans (7-9). At this point, the refutation of Julian begins in good earnest, and the method that he proposes to use is stated; viz., to adduce the adverse statements, and refute them one by one (10). Beginning at the beginning, he quotes first the title of the paper sent him, which declares that it is directed against "those who condemn matrimony, and ascribe its fruit to the Devil" (11), which certainly, says Augustine, does not describe him or the catholics. The next twenty chapters (10-30), accordingly, following Julian's order, labour to prove that marriage is good, and ordained by God, but that its good includes fecundity indeed, but not concupiscence, which arose from sin, and contracts sin. It is next argued, that the doctrine of original sin does not imply an evil origin for man (31-51); and in the course of this argument, the following propositions are especially defended: that God makes offspring for good and bad alike, just as He sends the rain and sunshine on just and unjust (31-34); that God makes everything to be found in marriage except its flaw, concupiscence (35-40); that marriage is not the cause of original sin, but only the channel through which it is transmitted (41-47); and that to assert that evil cannot arise from what is good leaves us in the clutches of that very Manicheism which is so unjustly charged against the catholics-for, if evil be not eternal, what else was there from which it could arise but something good? (48-51). In concluding, Augustine recapitulates, and argues especially, that shameful concupiscence is of sin, and the author of sin, and was not in paradise (52-54); that children are made by God, and only marred by the Devil (55); that Julian, in admitting that Christ died for infants, admits that they need salvation (56); that what the Devil makes in children is not a substance, but an injury to a substance (57-58); and that to suppose that concupiscence existed in any form in paradise introduces incongruities in our conception of life in that abode of primeval bliss (59-60).

The long and important treatise, Against Two Letters of the Pelagians, consists of four books, the first of which replies to the letter sent to Rome, and the other three to that sent to Thessalonica. After a short introduction, in which he thanks Boniface for his kindness, and gives reasons why heretical writings should be answered (1-3), Augustine begins at once to rebut the calumnies which the letter before him brings against the catholics (4-28). These are seven in number: 1. That the catholics destroy free will; to which Augustine replies that none are "forced into sin by the necessity of their flesh," but all sin by free will, though no man can have a righteous will save by God's grace, and that it is really the Pelagians that destroy free will by exaggerating it (4-8); 2. That Augustine declares that such marriage as now exists is not of God (9); 3. That sexual desire and intercourse are made a device of the Devil, which is sheer Manicheism (10-11); 4. That the Old-Testament saints are said to have died in sin (12); 5. That Paul and the other apostles are asserted to have been polluted by lust all their days; Augustine's answer to which includes a running commentary on Rom. vii. 7 sq., in which (correcting his older exegesis) he shows that Paul is giving here a transcript of his own experience as a typical Christian (13-24); 6. That Christ is said not to have been free from sin (25); 7. That baptism does not give complete remission of sins, but leaves roots from which they may again grow; to which Augustine replies that baptism does remit all sins, but leaves concupiscence, which, although not sin, is the source of sin (26-28). Next, the positive part of Julian's letter is taken up, and his profession of faith against the catholics examined (29-41). The seven affirmations that Julian makes here are designed as the obverse of the seven charges against the catholics. He believed: 1. That free will is in all by nature, and could not perish by Adam's sin (29); 2. That marriage, as now existent, was ordained by God (30); 3. That sexual impulse and virility are from God, (31-35); 4. That men are God's work, and no one is forced to do good or evil unwillingly, but are assisted by grace to good, and incited by the Devil to evil (36-38); 5. That the saints of the Old Testament were perfected in righteousness here, and so passed into eternal life (39); 6. That the grace of Christ (ambiguously meant) is necessary for all, and all children-even those of baptized parents-are to be baptized (40); 7. And that baptism gives full cleansing from all sins; to which Augustine pointedly asks, "What does it do for infants, then?" (41). The book concludes with an answer to Julian's conclusion, in which he demands a general council, and charges the catholics with Manicheism.

The second, third, and fourth books deal with the letter to Rufus in a somewhat similar way, the second and third books being occupied with the calumnies brought against the catholics, and the fourth with the claims made by the Pelagians. The second begins by repelling the charge of Manicheism brought against the catholics (1-4), to which the pointed remark is added, that the Pelagians cannot hope to escape condemnation because they are willing to condemn another heresy; and then defends (with less success) the Roman clergy against the charge of prevarication in their dealing with the Pelagians (5-8), in the course of which all that can be said in defence of Zosimus' wavering policy is said well and strongly. Next the charges against catholic teaching are taken up and answered (9-16), especially the two important accusations that they maintain fate under the name of grace (9-12), and that they make God an "accepter of persons" (13-16). Augustine's replies to these charges are in every way admirable. The charge of "fate" rests solely on the catholic denial that grace is given according to preceding merits; but the Pelagians do not escape the same charge when they acknowledge that the "fates" of baptized and unbaptized infants do differ. It is, in truth, not a question of "fate," but of gratuitous bounty; and "it is not the catholics that assert fate under the name of grace, but the Pelagians that choose to call divine grace by the name of `fate' "(12). As to "acceptance of persons," we must define what we mean by that. God certainly does not accept one's "person" above another's; He does not give to one rather than to another because He sees something to please Him in one rather than another: quite the opposite. He gives of His bounty to one while giving all their due to all, as in the parable (Matt. xx. 9 sq.) To ask why He does this, is to ask in vain: the apostle answers by not answering (Rom. ix.); and before the dumb infants, who are yet made to differ, all objection to God is dumb. From this point, the book becomes an examination of the Pelagian doctrine of prevenient merit (17-23), concluding that God gives all by grace from the beginning to the end of every process of doing good. 1. He commands the good; 2. He gives the desire to do it; and, 3. He gives the power to do it: and all, of His gratuitous mercy. The third book continues the discussion of the calumnies of the Pelagians against the catholics, and enumerates and answers six of them: viz., that the catholics teach, 1. That the Old-Testament law was given, not to justify the obedient, but to serve as cause of greater sin (2-3); 2. That baptism does not give entire remission of sins, but the baptized are partly God's and partly the Devil's (4-5); 3. That the Holy Ghost did not assist virtue in the Old Testament (6-13); 4. That the Bible saints were not holy, but only less wicked than others (14-15); 5. That Christ was a sinner by necessity of His flesh (doubtless, Julian's inference from the doctrine of race-sin) (16); 6. That men will begin to fulfil God's commandments only after the resurrection (17-23). Augustine shows that at the basis of all these calumnies lies either misapprehension or misrepresentation; and, in concluding the book, enumerates the three chief points in the Pelagian heresy, with the five claims growing out of them, of which they most boasted, and then elucidates the mutual relations of the three parties, catholics, Pelagians, and Manicheans, with reference to these points, showing that the catholics stand asunder from both the others, and condemn both (24-27). This conclusion is really a preparation for the fourth book, which takes up these five Pelagian claims, and, after showing the catholic position on them all in brief (1-3), discusses them in turn (4-19): viz., the praise of the creature (4-8), the praise of marriage (9), the praise of the law (10-11), the praise of free will (12-16), and the praise of the saints (17-18). At the end, Augustine calls on the Pelagians to cease to oppose the Manicheans, only to fall into as bad heresy as theirs (19); and then, in reply to their accusation that the catholics were proclaiming novel doctrine, he adduces the testimony of Cyprian and Ambrose, both of whom had received Pelagius' praise, on each of the three main points of Pelagianism (20-32), and then closes with the declaration that the "impious and foolish doctrine," as they called it, of the catholics, is immemorial truth (33), and with a denial of the right of the Pelagians to ask for a general council to condemn them (34). All heresies do not need an ecumenical synod for their condemnation; usually it is best to stamp them out locally, and not allow what may be confined to a corner to disturb the whole world.

These books were written late in 420, or early in 421, and Alypius appears to have conveyed them to Italy during the latter year. Before its close, Augustine, having obtained and read the whole of Julian's attack on the first book of his work On Marriage and Concupiscence, wrote out a complete answer to it, -a task that he was all the more anxious to complete, on perceiving that the extracts sent by Valerius were not only all from the first book of Julian's treatise, but were somewhat altered in the extracting. The resulting work, Against Julian, one of the longest that he wrote in the whole course of the Pelagian controversy, shows its author at his best: according to Cardinal Noris's judgment, he appears in it "almost divine," and Augustine himself clearly set great store by it. In the first book of this noble treatise, after professing his continued love for Julian, "whom he was unable not to love, whatever he [Julian] should say against him" (35), he undertakes to show that in affixing the opprobrious name of Manicheans on those who assert original sin, Julian is incriminating many of the most famous fathers, both of the Latin and Greek Churches. In proof of this, he makes appropriate quotations from Irenaeus, Cyprian, Reticius, Olympius, Hilary, Ambrose, Gregory Nazianzenus, Basil, John of Constantinople. Then he argues, that, so far from the catholics falling into Manichean heresy, Julian plays, himself, into the hands of the Manicheans in their strife against the catholics, by many unguarded statements, such as, e.g., when he says that an evil thing cannot arise from what is good, that the work of the Devil cannot be suffered to be diffused by means of a work of God, that a root of evil cannot be placed within a gift of God, and the like. The second book advances to greater detail, and adduces the five great arguments which the Pelagians urged against the catholics, in order to test them by the voice of antiquity. These arguments are stated as follows (2): "For you say, `That we, by asserting original sin, affirm that the Devil is the maker of infants, condemn marriage, deny that all sins are remitted in baptism, accuse God of the guilt of sin, and produce despair of perfection.' You contend that all these are consequences, if we believe that infants are born bound by the sin of the first man, and are therefore under the Devil unless they are born again in Christ. For, `It is the Devil that creates,' you say, `if they are created from that wound which the Devil inflicted on the human nature that was made at first.' `And marriage is condemned,' you say, `if it is to be believed to have something about it whence it produces those worthy of condemnation.' `And all sins are not remitted in baptism,' you say, `if there remains any evil in baptized couples whence evil offspring are produced.' `And how is God,' you ask, `not unjust, if He, while remitting their own sins to baptized persons, yet condemns their offspring, inasmuch as, although it is created by Him, it yet ignorantly and involuntarily contracts the sins of others from those very parents to whom they are remitted?' `Nor can men believe,' you add, `that virtue-to which corruption is to be understood to be contrary-can be perfected, if they cannot believe that it can destroy the

inbred vices, although, no doubt, these can scarcely be considered vices, since he does not sin, who is unable to be other than he was created.'
"These arguments are then tested, one by one, by the authority of the earlier teachers who were appealed to in the first book, and shown to be condemned by them. The remaining four books follow Julian's four books, argument by argument, refuting him in detail. In the third book it is urged that although God is good, and made man good, and instituted marriage which is, therefore, good, nevertheless concupiscence is evil, and in it the flesh lusts against the spirit. Although chaste spouses use this evil well, continent believers do better in not using it at all. It is pointed out, how far all this is from the madness of the Manicheans, who dream of matter as essentially evil and co-eternal with God; and shown that evil concupiscence sprang from Adam's disobedience and, being transmitted to us, can be removed only by Christ. It is shown, also, that Julian himself confesses lust to be evil, inasmuch as he speaks of remedies against it, wishes it to be bridled, and speaks of the continent waging a glorious warfare. The fourth book follows the second book of Julian's work, and makes two chief contentions: that unbelievers have no true virtues, and that even the heathen recognize concupiscence as evil. It also argues that grace is not given according to merit, and yet is not to be confounded with fate; and explains the text that asserts that 'God wishes all men to be saved,' in the sense that 'all men' means 'all that are to be saved' since none are saved except by His will. The fifth book, in like manner, follows Julian's third book, and treats of such subjects as these: that it is due to sin that any infants are lost; that shame arose in our first parents through sin; that sin can well be the punishment of preceding sin; that concupiscence is always evil, even in those who do not assent to it; that true marriage may exist without intercourse; that the "flesh" of Christ differs from the "sinful flesh" of other men; and the like. In the sixth book, Julian's fourth book is followed, and original sin is proved from the baptism of infants, the teaching of the apostles, and the rites of exorcism and exsufflation incorporated in the form of baptism. Then, by the help of the illustration drawn from the olive and the oleaster, it is explained how Christian parents can produce unregenerate offspring; and the originally voluntary character of sin is asserted, even though it now comes by inheritance.

After the completion of this important work, there succeeded a lull in the controversy, of some years duration; and the calm refutation of Pelagianism and exposition of Christian grace, which Augustine gave in his Enchiridion, might well have seemed to him his closing word on this all-absorbing subject. But he had not yet given the world all he had in treasure for it, and we can rejoice in the chance that five or six years afterwards drew from him a renewed discussion of some of the more important aspects of the doctrine of grace. The circumstances which brought this about are sufficiently interesting in themselves, and open up to us an unwonted view into the monastic life of the times. There was an important monastery at Adrumetum, the metropolitan city of the province of Byzacium, from which a monk named Florus went out on a journey of charity to his native country of Uzalis about 426. On the journey he met with Augustine's letter to Sixtus, in which the doctrines of gratuitous and prevenient grace were expounded. He was much delighted with it, and, procuring a copy, sent it back to his monastery for the edification of his brethren, while he himself went on to Carthage. At the monastery, the letter created great disturbance: without the knowledge of the abbot, Valentinus, it was read aloud to the monks, many of whom were unskilled in theological questions; and some five or more were greatly offended, and declared that free will was destroyed by it. A secret strife arose among the brethren, some taking extreme grounds on both sides. Of all this, Valentinus remained ignorant until the return of Florus, who was attacked as the author of all the trouble, and who felt it his duty to inform the abbot of the state of affairs. Valentinus applied first to the bishop, Evodius, for such instruction as would make Augustine's letter clear to the most simple. Evodius replied, praising their zeal and deprecating their contentiousness, and explaining that Adam had full free will, but that it is now wounded and weak, and Christ's mission was as a physician to cure and recuperate it. "Let them read," is his prescription, "the words of God's elders....And when they do not understand, let them not quickly reprehend, but pray to understand." This did not, however, cure the malecontents, and the holy presbyter Sabrinus was appealed to, and sent a book with clear interpretations. But neither was this satisfactory; and Valentinus, at last, reluctantly consented that Augustine himself should be consulted—fearing, he says, lest by making inquiries he should seem to waver about the truth. Two members of the community were consequently permitted to journey to Hippo, but they took with them no introduction and no commendation from their abbot. Augustine, nevertheless, received them without hesitation, as they bore themselves with too great simplicity to allow him to suspect them of deception. Now we get a glimpse of life in the great bishop's monastic home. The monks told their story, and were listened to with courtesy and instructed with patience; and, as they were anxious to get home before Easter, they received a letter for Valentinus in which Augustine briefly explains the nature of the misapprehension that had arisen, and points out that both grace and free will must be defended, and neither so exaggerated as to deny the other. The letter of Sixtus, he explains, was written against the Pelagians, who assert that grace is given according to merit, and briefly expounds the true doctrine of grace as necessarily gratuitous and therefore prevenient. When the monks were on the point of starting home, they were joined by a third companion from Adrumetum, and were led to prolong their visit. This gave him the opportunity he craved for their fuller instruction: he read with them and explained to them not only his letter to Sixtus, from which the strife had risen, but much of the chief literature of the Pelagian controversy, copies of which also were made for them to take home with them; and when they were ready to go, he sent by them another and longer letter to Valentinus, and placed in their hands a treatise composed for their especial use, which, moreover, he explained to them. This longer letter is essentially an exhortation "to turn aside neither to the right hand nor to the left,"-neither to the left hand of the Pelagian error of upholding free will in such a manner as to deny grace, nor to the right hand of the equal error of so upholding grace as if we might yield ourselves to evil with impunity. Both grace and free will are to be proclaimed; and it is true both that grace is not given to merits, and that we are to be judged at the last day according to our works. The treatise which Augustine composed for a fuller exposition of these doctrines is the important work On Grace and Free Will. After a brief introduction, explaining the occasion of his writing, and exhorting the monks to humility and teachableness before God's revelations (1), Augustine begins by asserting and proving the two propositions that the Scriptures clearly teach that man has free will (2-5), and, as clearly, the necessity of grace for doing any good (6-9). He then examines the passages which the Pelagians claim as teaching that we must first turn to God, before He visits us with His grace (10-11), and then undertakes to show that grace is not given to merit (12 sq.), appealing especially to Paul's teaching and example, and replying to the assertion that forgiveness is the only grace that is not given according to our merits (15-18), and to the query, "How can eternal life be both of grace and of reward?" (19-21). The nature of grace, what it is, is next explained (22 sq.). It is not the law, which gives only knowledge of sin (22-24), nor nature, which would render Christ's death needless (25), nor mere forgiveness of sins, as the Lord's Prayer (which should be read with Cyprian's comments on it) is enough to show (26). Nor will it do to say that it is given to the merit of a good will, thus distinguishing the good work which is of grace from the good will which precedes grace (27-30); for the Scriptures oppose this, and our prayers for others prove that we expect God to be the first mover, as indeed both Scripture and experience prove that He is. It is next shown that both free will and grace are concerned in the heart's conversion (31-32), and that love is the spring of all good in man (33-40), which, however, we have only because God first loved us (38), and which is certainly greater than knowledge, although the Pelagians admit only the latter to be from God (40). God's sovereign government of men's wills is then proved from Scripture (41-43), and the wholly gratuitous character of grace is illustrated (44), while the only possible theodicy is found in the certainty that the Lord of all the earth will do right. For, though no one knows why He takes one and leaves another, we all know that He hardens judicially and saves graciously—that He hardens none who do not deserve hardening, but none that He saves deserve to be saved (45). The treatise closes with an exhortation to its prayerful and repeated study (46).

The one request that Augustine made, on sending this work to Valentinus, was that Florus, through whom the controversy had arisen, should be sent to him, that he might converse with him and learn whether he had been misunderstood, or himself had misunderstood Augustine. In due time Florus arrived at Hippo, bringing a letter from Valentinus which addresses Augustine as "Lord Pope" (domine papa), thanks him for his "sweet" and "healing" instruction, and introduces Florus as one whose true faith could be confided in. It is very clear, both from Valentinus' letter and from the hints that Augustine gives, that his loving dealing with the monks had borne admirable fruit: "none were cast down for the worse, some were built up for the better." But it was reported to him that some one at the monastery had objected to the doctrine he had taught them, that "no man ought, then, to be rebuked for not keeping God's commandments; but only God should be besought that he might keep them." In other words, it was said that if all good was, in the last resort, from God's grace, man ought not to be blamed for not doing what he could not do, but God ought to be besought to do for man what He alone could do: we ought, in a word, to apply to the source of power. This occasioned the composition of yet another treatise On Rebuke and Grace, the object of which was to explain the relations of grace to human conduct, and especially to make it plain that the sovereignty of God's grace does not supersede our duty to ourselves or our fellow-men. It begins by thanking Valentinus for his letter and for sending Florus (whom Augustine finds well instructed in the truth), thanking God for the good effect of the previous book, and recommending its continued study, and then by briefly expounding the Catholic faith concerning grace, free-will, and the law (1-2). The general proposition that is defended is that the gratuitous sovereignty of God's grace does not supersede human means for obtaining and continuing it (3 sq.) This is shown by the apostle's example, who used all human means for the prosecution of his work, and yet confessed that it was "God that gave the increase" (3). Objections are then answered (4 sq.)—especially the great one that "it is not my fault if I do not do what I have not received grace for doing" (6); to which Augustine replies (7-10), that we deserve rebuke for our very unwillingness to be rebuked, that on the same reasoning the prescription of the law and the preaching of the gospel would be useless, that the apostle's example opposes such a position, and that our consciousness witnesses that we deserve rebuke for not persevering in the right way. From this point an important discussion arises, in this interest, of the gift of perseverance (11-19), and of God's election (20-24); the teaching being that no one is saved who does not persevere, and all that are predestinated or "called according to the purpose" (Augustine's phrase for what we should call "effectual calling") will persevere, and yet that we co-operate by our will in all good deeds, and deserve rebuke if we do not. Whether Adam received the gift of perseverance, and, in general, the difference between the grace given to him, which was that grace by which he could stand) and that now given to God's children (which is that grace by which we are actually made to stand), are next discussed (26-38), with the result of showing the superi-

or greatness of the gifts of grace now to those given before the fall. The necessity of God's mercy at all times, and our constant dependence on it, are next vigorously asserted (39-42); even in the day of judgment, if we are not judged "with mercy" we cannot be saved (41). The treatise is brought to an end by a concluding application of the whole discussion to the special matter in hand, rebuke (43-49). Seeing that rebuke is one of God's means of working out his gracious purposes, it cannot be inconsistent with the sovereignty of that grace; for, of course, God predestinates the means with the end (43). Nor can we know, in our ignorance, whether our rebuke is, in any particular case, to be the means of amendment or the ground of greater condemnation. How dare we, then, withhold it? Let it be, however, graduated to the fault, and let us always remember its purpose (46-48). Above all, let us not dare hold it back, lest we hold back from our brother the means of his recovery, and, as well, disobey the command of God (49).

It was not long afterwards (about 427) when Augustine was called upon to attempt to reclaim a Carthaginian brother, Vitalis by name, who had been brought to trial on the charge of teaching that the beginning of faith was not the gift of God, but the act of man's own free will (ex propria voluntatis). This was essentially the semi-Pelagian position which was subsequently to make so large a figure in history; and Augustine treats it now as necessarily implying the basal idea of Pelagianism. In the important letter which he sent to Vitalis, he first argues that his position is inconsistent with the prayers of the church. He, Augustine, prays that Vitalis may come to the true faith; but does not this prayer ascribe the origination of right faith to God? The Church so prays for all men: the priest at the altar exhorts the people to pray God for unbelievers, that He may convert them to the faith; for catechumens, that He may breathe into them a desire for regeneration; for the faithful, that by His aid they may persevere in what they have begun: will Vitalis refuse to obey these exhortations, because, forsooth, faith is of free will and not of God's gift? Nay, will a Carthaginian scholar array himself against Cyprian's exposition of the Lord's Prayer? for he certainly teaches that we are to ask of God what Vitalis says is to be had of ourselves. We may go farther: it is not Cyprian, but Paul, who says, "Let us pray to God that we do no evil" (2 Cor. xiii. 7); it is the Psalmist who says, "The steps of man are directed by God" (Ps. xxxvi. 23). "If we wish to defend free will, let us not strive against that by which it is made free. For he who strives against grace, by which the will is made free for refusing evil and doing good, wishes his will to remain captive. Tell us, I beg you, how the apostle can say, 'We give thanks to the Father who made us fit to have our lot with the saints in light, who delivered us from the power of darkness, and translated us into the kingdom of the Son of His love' (Col. i. 12, 13), if not He, but itself, frees our choice? It is, then, a false rendering of thanks to God, as if He does what He does not do; and he has erred who has said that 'He makes us fit, etc.' 'The grace of God,' therefore, does not consist in the nature of free-will, and in law and teaching, as the Pelagian perversity dreams; but it is given for each single act by His will, concerning whom it is written,"- quoting Ps. lxvii. 10. About the middle of the letter, Augustine lays down twelve propositions against the Pelagians, which are important as communicating to us what he thought, at the end of the controversy, were the chief points in dispute. "Since, therefore," he writes, "we are catholic Christians: 1. We know that new-born children have not yet done anything in their own lives, good or evil, neither have they come into the miseries of this life according to the deserts of some previous life, which none of them can have had in their own persons; and yet, because they are born carnally after Adam, they contract the contagion of ancient death, by the first birth, and are not freed from the punishment of eternal death (which is contracted by a just condemnation, passing over from one to all), except they are by grace born again in Christ. 2. We know that the grace of God is given neither to children nor to adults according to our deserts. 3. We know that it is given to adults for each several act. 4. We know that it is not given to all men; and to those to whom it is given, it is not only not given according to the merits of works, but it is not even given to them according to the merits of their will; and this is especially apparent in children. 5. We know that to those to whom it is given, it is given by the gratuitous mercy of God. 6. We know that to those to whom it is not given, it is not given by the just judgment of God. 7. We know that we shall all stand before the tribunal of Christ, and each shall receive according to what he has done through the body—not according to what he would have done, had he lived longer—whether good or evil. 8. We know that even children are to receive according to what they have done through the body, whether good or evil. But according to what "they have done" not by their own act, but by the act of those by whose responses for them they are said both to renounce the Devil and to believe in God, wherefore they are counted among the number of the faithful, and have part in the statement of the Lord when He says, "Whosoever shall believe and be baptized, shall be saved." Therefore also, to those who do not receive this sacrament, belongs what follows, "But whosoever shall not have believed, shall be damned" (Mark xvi. 16). Whence these too, as I have said, if they die in that early age, are judged, of course, according to what they have done through the body, i.e., in the time in which they were in the body, when they believe or do not believe by the heart and mouth of their sponsors, when they are baptized or not baptized, when they eat or do not eat the flesh of Christ, when they drink or do not drink His blood—according to those things, then, which they have done through the body, not according to those which, had they lived longer, they would have done. 9. We know that blessed are the dead that die in the Lord; and that what they would have done had they lived longer, is not imputed to them. 10. We know that those that believe, with their own heart, in the Lord, do so by their own free will and choice. 11. We know that we who already believe act with right faith towards those who do not wish to believe, when we pray to God that they may wish it. 12. We know that for those who have believed out of this number, we both ought and are rightly and truly accustomed to return thanks to God, as for his benefits." Certainly such a body of propositions commends their author to us as Christian both in head and heart: they are admirable in every respect; and even in the matter of the salvation of infants, where he had not yet seen the light of truth, he expresses himself in a way as engaging in its hearty faith in God's goodness as it is honorable in its loyalty to what he believed to be truth and justice. Here his doctrine of the Church ran athwart and clouded his view of the reach of grace; but we seem to see between the lines the promise of the brighter dawn of truth that was yet to come. The rest of the epistle is occupied with an exposition and commendation of these propositions, which ranks with the richest passages of the anti-Pelagian writings, and which breathes everywhere a yearning for his correspondent which we cannot help hoping proved salutary to his faith.

It is not without significance, that the error of Vitalis took a semi-Pelagian form. Pure Pelagianism was by this time no longer a living issue. Augustine was himself, no doubt, not yet done with it. The second book of his treatise On Marriage and Concupiscence, which seems to have been taken to Italy by Alypius, in 421, received at once the attention of Julian, and was elaborately answered by him, during that same year, in eight books addressed to Florus. But Julian was now in Cilicia, and his book was slow in working its way westward. It was found at Rome by Alypius, apparently in 427 or 428, and he at once set about transcribing it for his friend's use. An opportunity arising to send it to Africa before it was finished, he forwarded to Augustine the five books that were ready, with an urgent request that they should receive his immediate attention, and a promise to send the other three as soon as possible. Augustine gives an account of his progress in his reply to them in a letter written to Quodvultdeus, apparently in 428. This deacon was urging Augustine to give the Church a succinct account of all heresies; and Augustine excuses himself from immediately undertaking that task by the press of work on his hands. He was writing his Retractations, and had already finished two books of them, in which he had dealt with two hundred and thirty-two works. His letters and homilies remained and he had given the necessary reading to many of the letters. Also, he tells his correspondent, he was engaged on a reply to the eight books of Julian's new work. Working night and day, he had already completed his response to the first three of Julian's books, and had begun on the fourth while still expecting the arrival of the last three which Alypius had promised to send. If he had completed the answer to the five books of Julian which he already had in hand, before the other three reached him, he might begin the work which Quodvultdeus so earnestly desired him to undertake. In due time, whatever may have been the trials and labours that needed first to be met, the desired treatise On Heresies was written (about 428), and the eighty-eighth chapter of it gives us a welcome compressed account of the Pelagian heresy, which may be accepted as the obverse of the account of catholic truth given in the letter to Vitalis. But the composition of this work was not the only interruption which postponed the completion of the second elaborate work against Julian. It was in the providence of God that the life of this great leader in the battle for grace should be prolonged until he could deal with semi-Pelagianism also. Information as to the rise of this new form of the heresy at Marseilles and elsewhere in Southern Gaul was conveyed to Augustine along with entreaties, that, as "faith's great patron," he would give his aid towards meeting it, by two laymen with whom he had already had correspondence—Prosper and Hilary They pointed out the difference between the new party and thorough-going Pelagianism; but, at the same time, the essentially Pelagianizing character of its formative elements. Its representatives were ready, as a rule, to admit that all men were lost in Adam, and no one could recover himself by his own free will, but all needed God's grace for salvation. But they objected to the doctrines of prevenient and of irresistible grace; and asserted that man could initiate the process of salvation by turning first to God, that all men could resist God's grace, and no grace could be given which they could not reject, and especially they denied that the gifts of grace came irrespective of merits, actual or foreseen. They said that what Augustine taught as to the calling of God's elect according to His own purpose was tantamount to fatalism, was contrary to the teaching of the fathers and the true Church doctrine, and, even if true, should not be preached, because of its tendency to drive men into indifference or despair. Hence, Prosper especially desired Augustine to point out the dangerous nature of these views, and to show that prevenient and co-operating grace is not inconsistent with free will, that God's predestination is not founded on foresight of receptivity in its objects, and that the doctrines of grace may be preached without danger to souls.

Augustine's answer to these appeals was a work in two books, On the Predestination of the Saints , the second book of which is usually known under the separate title of The Gift of Perseverance . The former book begins with a careful discrimination of the position of his new opponents they have made a right beginning in that they believe in original sin, and acknowledge that none are saved from it save by Christ, and that God's grace leads men's wills, and without grace no one can suffice for good deeds. These things will furnish a good starting-point for their progress to an acceptance of predestination also (1-2). The first question that needs discussion in such circumstances is, whether God gives the very beginnings of faith (3 sq.); since they admit that what Augustine had previously urged sufficed to prove that faith was the gift of God so far as that the increase of faith was given by Him, but not so far but that the beginning of faith may be understood to be man's, to which, then, God adds all other gifts (compare 43). Augustine insists that this is no other than the Pelagian assertion of grace according to merit (3), is opposed to Scripture (4-5), and begets arrogant boasting in ourselves (6). He replies to the objection that he had himself once held this view, by confessing it, and explaining that he was converted from it by 1 Cor. iv. 7, as applied by Cyprian (7-8), and expounds that verse as containing in its narrow compass a sufficient answer to the present theories (9-11). He answers, further, the objection that the apostle distinguishes faith from works, and works alone are meant in such passages, by pointing to John vi. 28, and similar statements in Paul (12-16). Then he answers the objection that he himself had previously taught that God acted on foresight of faith, by showing that he was misunderstood (17-18). He next shows that no objection lies against predestination that does not lie with equal force against grace (19-22)—since predestination is nothing but God's foreknowledge of and preparation for grace, and all questions of sovereignty and the like belong to grace. Did God not know to whom he was going to give faith (19)? or did he promise the results of faith, works, without promising the faith without which, as going before, the works were impossible? Would not this place God's fulfilment of his promise out of His power, and make it depend on man (20)? Why are men more willing to trust in their weakness than in God's strength? do they count God's promises more uncertain than their own performance (22)? He next proves the sovereignty of grace, and of predestination, which is but the preparation for grace, by the striking examples of infants, and, above all, of the human nature of Christ (23-31), and then speaks of the twofold calling, one external and one "according to purpose,"-the latter of which is efficacious and sovereign (32-37). In closing, the semi-Pelagian position is carefully defined and refuted as opposed, alike with the grosser Pelagianism, to the Scriptures of both Testaments (38-42).

The purpose of the second book, which has come down to us under the separate title of On the Gift of Perseverance, is to show that that perseverance which endures to the end is as much of God as the beginning of faith, and that no man who has been "called according to God's purpose," and has received this gift, can fall from grace and be lost. The first half of the treatise is devoted to this theme (1-33). It begins by distinguishing between temporary perseverance, which endures for a time, and that which continues to the end (1), and affirms that the latter is certainly a gift of God's grace, and is, therefore, asked from God which would otherwise be but a mocking petition (2-3). This, the Lord's Prayer itself might teach us, as under Cyprian's exposition it does teach us—each petition being capable of being read as a prayer for perseverance (4-9). Of course, moreover, it cannot be lost, otherwise it would not be "to the end." If man forsakes God, of course it is he that does it, and he is doubtless under continual temptation to do so; but if he abides with God, it is God who secures that, and God is equally able to keep one when drawn to Him, as He is to draw him to Him (10-15). He argues anew at this point, that grace is not according to merit, but always in mercy; and explains and illustrates the unsearchable ways of God in His sovereign but merciful dealing with men (16-25), and closes this part of the treatise by a defence of himself against adverse quotations from his early work on Free Will, which he has already corrected in his Retractations. The second half of the book discusses the objections that were being urged against the preaching of predestination (34-62), as if it opposed and enervated the preaching of the Gospel. He replies that Paul and the apostles, and Cyprian and the fathers, preached both together; that the same objections will lie against the preaching of God's foreknowledge and grace itself, and, indeed, against preaching any of the virtues, as, e.g., obedience, while declaring them God's gifts. He meets the objections in detail, and shows that such preaching is food to the soul, and must not be withheld from men; but explains that it must be given gently, wisely, and prayerfully. The whole treatise ends with an appeal to the prayers of the Church as testifying that all good is from God (63-65), and to the great example of unmerited grace and sovereign predestination in the choice of one human nature without preceding merit, to be united in one person with the Eternal Word—an illustration of his theme of the gratuitous grace of God which he is never tired of adducing (66-67).

These books were written in 428-429, and after their completion the unfinished work against Julian was resumed. Alypius had sent the remaining three books, and Augustine slowly toiled on to the end of his reply to the sixth book. But he was to be interrupted once more, and this time by the most serious of all interruptions. On the 28th of August, 430, with the Vandals thundering at the gates of Hippo, full of good works and of faith, he turned his face away from the strifes-whether theological or secular-of earth, and entered into rest with the Lord whom he loved. The last work against Julian was already one of the most considerable in size of all his books; but it was never finished, and retains until to-day the significant title of The Unfinished Work. Augustine had hesitated to undertake this work, because he found Julian's arguments too silly either to deserve refutation, or to afford occasion for really edifying discourse. And certainly the result falls below Augustine's usual level, though this is not due, as is so often said, to failing powers and great age; for nothing that he wrote surpasses in mellow beauty and chastened strength the two books, On the Predestination of the Saints, which were written after four books of this work were completed. The plan of the work is to state Julian's arguments in his own words, and follow it with his remarks; thus giving it something of the form of a dialogue. It follows Julian's work, book by book. The first book states and answers certain calumnies which Julian had brought against Augustine and the catholic faith on the ground of their confession of original sin. Julian had argued, that, since God is just, He cannot impute another's sins to innocent infants; since sin is nothing but evil will, there can be no sin in infants who are not yet in the use of their will; and, since the freedom of will that is given to man consists in the capacity of both sinning and not sinning, free will is denied to those who attribute sin to nature. Augustine replies to these arguments, and answers certain objections that are made to his work On Marriage and Concupiscence, and then corrects Julian's false explanations of certain Scriptures from John viii., Rom. vi., vii., and 2 Timothy. The second book is a discussion of Rom. v. 12, which Julian had tried, like the other Pelagians, to explain by the "imitation" of Adam's bad example. The third book examines the abuse by Julian of certain Old-Testament passages-in Deut. xxiv., 2 Kings xiv., Ezek. xviii.-in his effort to show that God does not impute the father's sins to the children; as well as his similar abuse of Heb. xi. The charge of Manicheism, which was so repetitiously brought by Julian against the catholics, is then examined and refuted. The fourth book treats of Julian's strictures on Augustine's On Marriage and Concupiscence ii. 4-11, and proves from 1 John ii. 16 that concupiscence is evil, and not the work of God, but of the Devil. He argues that the shame that accompanies it is due to its sinfulness, and that there was none of it in Christ; also, that infants are born obnoxious to the first sin, and proves the corruption of their origin from Wisd. x. 10, 11. The fifth book defends On Marriage and Concupiscence ii. 12 sq., and argues that a sound nature could not have shame on account of its members, and the need of regeneration for what is generated by means of shameful concupiscence. Then Julian's abuse of 1 Cor. xv., Rom. v., Matt. vii. 17 and 33, with reference to

On Marriage and Concupiscence ii. 14, 20, 26, is discussed; and then the origin of evil, and God's treatment of evil in the world. The sixth book traverses Julian's strictures on On Marriage and Concupiscence ii. 34 sq., and argues that human nature was changed for the worse by the sin of Adam, and thus was made not only sinful, but the source of sinners; and that the forces of free will by which man could at first do rightly if he wished, and refrain from sin if he chose, were lost by Adam's sin. He attacks Julian's definition of free will as "the capacity for sinning and not sinning" (possibilitas peccandi et non peccandi); and proves that the evils of this life are the punishment of sin—including, first of all, physical death. At the end, he treats of 1 Cor. xv. 22.

Although the great preacher of grace was taken away by death before the completion of this book, yet his work was not left incomplete. In the course of the next year (431) the Ecumenical Council of Ephesus condemned Pelagianism for the whole world; and an elaborate treatise against the pure Pelagianism of Julian was already in 430 an anachronism. Semi-Pelagianism was yet to run its course, and to work its way so into the heart of a corrupt church as not to be easily displaced; but Pelagianism was to die with the first generation of its advocates. As we look back now through the almost millennium and a half of years that has intervened since Augustine lived and wrote, it is to his Predestination of the Saints— a completed, and well-completed, treatise—and not to The Unfinished Work , that we look as the crown and completion of his labours for grace.

Part Four - The Theology of Grace

The theology which Augustine opposed, in his anti-Pelagian writings, to the errors of Pelagianism, is, shortly, the theology of grace. Its roots were planted deeply in his own experience, and in the teachings of Scripture, especially of that apostle whom he delights to call 'the great preacher of grace,' and to follow whom, in his measure, was his greatest desire. The grace of God in Jesus Christ, conveyed to us by the Holy Spirit and evidenced by the love that He sheds abroad in our hearts, is the centre around which this whole side of His system revolves, and the germ out of which it grows. He was the more able to make it thus central because of the harmony of this view of salvation with the general principle of his whole theology, which was theocentric and revolved around his conception of God as the immanent and vital spirit in whom all things live and move and have their being. In like manner, God is the absolute good, and all good is either Himself or from Him; and only as God makes us good, are we able to do anything good.

The necessity of grace to man, Augustine argued from the condition of the race as partakers of Adam's sin. God created man upright, and endowed him with human faculties, including free will; and gave to him freely that grace by which he was able to retain his uprightness. Being thus put on probation, with divine aid to enable him to stand if he chose, Adam used his free choice for sinning, and involved his whole race in his fall. It was on account of this sin that he died physically and spiritually, and this double death passes over from him to us. That all his descendants by ordinary generation are partakers in Adam's guilt and condemnation, Augustine is sure from the teachings of Scripture; and this is the fact of original sin, from which no one generated from Adam is free, and from which no one is freed save as regenerated in Christ. But how we are made partakers of it, he is less certain: sometimes he speaks as if it came by some mysterious unity of the race, so that we were all personally present in the individual Adam, and thus the whole race was the one man that sinned; sometimes he speaks more in the sense of modern realists, as if

Adam's sin corrupted the nature, and the nature now corrupts those to whom it is communicated; sometimes he speaks as if it were due to simple heredity; sometimes, again, as if it depended on the presence of shameful concupiscence in the act of procreation, so that the propagation of guilt depends on the propagation of offspring by means of concupiscence. However transmitted, it is yet a fact that sin is propagated, and all mankind became sinners in Adam. The result of this is that we have lost the divine image, though not in such a sense that no lineaments of it remain to us; and, the sinning soul making the flesh corruptible, our whole nature is corrupted, and we are unable to do anything of ourselves truly good. This includes, of course, an injury to our will. Augustine, writing for the popular eye, treats this subject in popular language. But it is clear that he distinguished, in his thinking, between will as a faculty and will in a broader sense. As a mere faculty, will is and always remains an indifferent thing — after the fall, as before it, continuing poised in indifferency, and ready, like a weathercock, to be turned whithersoever the breeze that blows from the heart ('will,' in the broader sense) may direct. It is not the faculty of willing, but the man who makes use of that faculty, that has suffered change from the fall. In paradise man stood in full ability: he had the posse non peccare, but not yet the non posse peccare; that is, he was endowed with a capacity for either part, and possessed the grace of God by which he was able to stand if he would, but also the power of free will by which he might fall if he would. By his fall he has suffered a change, is corrupt, and under the power of Satan; his will (in the broader sense) is now injured, wounded, diseased, enslaved, — although the faculty of will (in the narrow sense) remains indifferent. Augustine's criticism of Pelagius' discrimination of 'capacity' (possibilitas, posse), 'will' (voluntas, velle), and 'act' (actio, esse), does not turn on the discrimination itself, but on the incongruity of placing the power, ability in the mere capacity or possibility, rather than in the living agent who 'wills' and 'acts.' He himself adopts an essentially similar distribution, with only this correction; and thus keeps the faculty of will indifferent, but places the power of using it in the active agent, man. According, then, to the character of this man, will the use of the free will be. If the man be holy he will make a holy use of it, and if he be corrupt he will make a sinful use of it: if he be essentially holy, he cannot (like God Himself) make a sinful use of his will; and if he be enslaved to sin, he cannot make a good use of it. The last is the present condition of men by nature. They have free will; the faculty by which they act remains in indifferency, and they are allowed to use it just as they choose: but such as they cannot desire and therefore cannot choose anything but evil; and therefore they, and therefore their choice, and therefore their willing, is always evil and never good. They are thus the slaves of sin, which they obey; and while their free will avails for sinning, it does not avail for doing any good unless they be first freed by the grace of God. It is undeniable that this view is in consonance with modern psychology: let us once conceive of 'the will' as simply the whole man in the attitude of willing, and it is immediately evident, that, however abstractly free the 'will' is, it is conditioned and enslaved in all its action by the character of the willing agent: a bad man does not cease to be bad in the act of willing, and a good man remains good even in his acts of choice.

In its nature, grace is assistance, help from God; and all divine aid may be included under the term, — as well what may be called natural, as what may be called spiritual, aid, Spiritual grace includes, no doubt, all external help that God gives man for working out his salvation, such as the law, the preaching of the gospel, the example of Christ, by which we may learn the right way; it includes also forgiveness of sins, by which we are freed from the guilt already incurred; but above all it includes that help which God gives by His Holy Spirit, working within, not without, by which man is enabled to choose and to do what he sees, by the teachings of the law, or by the gospel, or by the natural conscience, to be right. Within this aid are included all those spiritual exercises which we call regeneration, justification, perseverance to the end, — in a word, all the divine assistance by which, in being made Christians, we are made to differ from other men. Augustine is fond of representing this grace as in essence the writing of God's law (or of God's will) on our hearts, so that it appears hereafter as our own desire and wish; and even more prevalently as the shedding abroad of love in our hearts by the Holy Ghost, given to us in Christ Jesus; therefore, as a change of disposition, by which we come to love and freely choose, in co-operation with God's aid, just the things which hitherto we have been unable to choose because in bondage to sin. Grace, thus, does not make void free will: it acts through free will, and acts upon it only by liberating it from its bondage to sin, i.e., by liberating the agent that uses the free will, so that he is no longer enslaved by his fleshly lusts, and is enabled to make use of his free will in choosing the good; and thus it is only by grace that free will is enabled to act in good part. But just because grace changes the disposition, and so enables man, hitherto enslaved to sin, for the first time to desire and use his free will for good, it lies in the very nature of the case that it is prevenient. Also, as the very name imports, it is necessarily gratuitous; since man is enslaved to sin until it is given, all the merits that he can have prior to it are bad merits, and deserve punishment, not gifts of favour. When, then, it is asked, on the ground of what, grace is given, it can only be answered, 'on the ground of God's infinite mercy and undeserved favour.' There is nothing in man to merit it, and it first gives merit of good to man. All men alike deserve death, and all that comes to them in the way of blessing is necessarily of God's free and unmerited favour. This is equally true of all grace. It is pre-eminently clear of that grace which gives faith, the root of all other graces, which is given of God, not to merits of good-will or incipient turning to Him, but of His sovereign good pleasure. But equally with faith, it is true of all other divine gifts: we may, indeed, speak of 'merits of good' as succeeding faith; but as all these merits find their root in faith, they are but 'grace on grace,' and men need God's mercy always, throughout this life, and even on the judgment day itself, when, if they are judged without mercy, they must be condemned. If we ask, then, why God gives grace, we can only answer that it is of His unspeakable mercy; and if we ask why He gives it to one rather than to another, what can we answer but that it is of His will? The sovereignty of grace results from its very gratuitousness: where none deserve it, it can be given only of the sovereign good pleasure of the great Giver, — and this is necessarily inscrutable, but cannot be unjust. We can faintly perceive, indeed, some reasons why God may be supposed not to have chosen to give His saving grace to all, or even to the most; but we cannot understand why He has chosen to give it to just the individuals to whom He has given it, and to withhold it from just those from whom He has withheld it. Here we are driven to the apostle's cry, 'Oh the depth of the riches both of the mercy and the justice of God!'

 The effects of grace are according to its nature. Taken as a whole, it is the recreative principle sent forth from God for the recovery of man from his slavery to sin, and for his reformation in the divine image. Considered as to the time of its giving, it is either operating or co-operating grace, i.e., either the grace that first enables the will to choose the good, or the grace that co-operates with the already enabled will to do the good; and it is, therefore, also called either prevenient or subsequent grace. It is not to be conceived of as a series of disconnected divine gifts, but as a constant efflux from God; but we may look upon it in the various steps of its operation in men, as bringing forgiveness of sins, faith, which is the beginning of all good, love to God, progressive power of good working, and perseverance to the end. In any case, and in all its operations alike, just because it is power from on high and the living spring of a new and re-created life, it is irresistible and indefectible. Those on whom the Lord bestows the gift of faith working from within, not from without, of course, have faith, and cannot help believing. Those to whom perseverance to the end is given must persevere to the end. It is not to be objected to this, that many seem to begin well who do not persevere: this also is of God, who has in such cases given great blessings indeed, but not this blessing, of perseverance to the end. Whatever of good men have, that God has given; and what they have not, why, of course, God has not given it. Nor can it be objected, that this leaves all uncertain: it is only unknown to us, but this is not uncertainty; we cannot know that we are to have any gift which God sovereignly gives, of course, until it is given, and we therefore cannot know that we have perseverance unto the end until we actually persevere to the end; but who would call what God does, and knows He is to do, uncertain, and what man is to do certain? Nor will it do to say that thus nothing is left for us to do: no doubt, all things are in God's hands, and we should praise God that this is so, but we must co-operate with Him; and it is just because it is He that is working in us the willing and the doing, that it is worth our while to work out our salvation with fear and trembling. God has not determined the end without determining the appointed means.

Now, Augustine argues, since grace certainly is gratuitous, and given to no preceding merits, — prevenient and antecedent to all good, — and, therefore, sovereign, and bestowed only on those whom God selects for its reception; we must, of course, believe that the eternal God has foreknown all this from the beginning. He would be something less than God, had He not foreknown that He intended to bestow this prevenient, gratuitous, and sovereign grace on some men, and had He not foreknown equally the precise individuals on whom He intended to bestow it. To foreknow is to prepare beforehand. And this is predestination. He argues that there can be no objection to predestination, in itself considered, in the mind of any man who believes in a God: what men object to is the gratuitous and sovereign grace to which no additional difficulty is added by the necessary assumption that it was foreknown and prepared or from eternity. That predestination does not proceed on the foreknowledge of good or of faith, follows from its being nothing more than the foresight and preparation of grace, which, in its very idea, is gratuitous and not according to any merits, sovereign and according only to God's purpose, prevenient and in order to faith and good works. It is the sovereignty of grace, not its foresight or the preparation for it, which places men in God's hands, and suspends salvation absolutely on his unmerited mercy. But just because God is God, of course, no one receives grace who has not been foreknown and afore-selected for the gift; and, as much of course, no one who has been foreknown and afore-selected for it, fails to receive it. Therefore the number of the predestinated is fixed, and fixed by God. Is this fate? Men may call God's grace fate if they choose; but it is not fate, but undeserved love and tender mercy, without which none would be saved. Does it paralyze effort? Only to those who will not strive to obey God because obedience is His gift. Is it unjust? Far from it: shall not God do what He will with His own undeserved favour? It is nothing but gratuitous mercy, sovereignly distributed, and foreseen and provided for from all eternity by Him who has selected us in His Son.

When Augustine comes to speak of the means of grace, i.e., of the channels and circumstances of its conference to men, he approaches the meeting point of two very dissimilar streams of his theology — his doctrine of grace and his doctrine of the Church — and he is sadly deflected from the natural course of his theology by the alien influence. He does not, indeed, bind the conference of grace to the means in such a sense that the grace must be given at the exact time of the application of the means. He does not deny that 'God is able, even when no man rebukes, to correct whom He will, and to lead him on to the wholesome mortification of repentance by the most hidden and most mighty power of His medicine.' Though the Gospel must be known in order that man may be saved (for how shall they believe without a preacher?), yet the preacher is nothing, and the preachment is nothing, but God only that gives the increase. He even has something like a distant glimpse of what has since been called the distinction between the visible and invisible Church — speaking of men not yet born as among those who are 'called according to God's purpose,' and, therefore, of the saved who constitute the Church — asserting that those who are so called, even before they believe, are 'already children of God enrolled in the memorial of their Father with unchangeable surety,' and, at the same time; allowing that there are many already in the visible Church who are not of it, and who can therefore depart from it. But he teaches that those who are thus lost out of the visible Church are lost because of some fatal flaw in their baptism, or on account of post-baptismal sins; and that those who are of the 'called according to the purpose' are predestinated not only to salvation, but to salvation by baptism. Grace is not tied to the means in the sense that it is not conferred save in the means; but it is tied to the means in the sense that it is not conferred without the means. Baptism, for instance, is absolutely necessary for salvation: no exception is allowed except such as save the principle — baptism of blood (martyrdom), and, somewhat grudgingly, baptism of intention. And baptism, when worthily received, is absolutely efficacious: 'if a man were to die immediately after baptism, he would have nothing at all left to hold him liable to punishment.' In a word, while there are many baptized who will not be saved, there are none saved who have not been baptized; it is the grace of God that saves, but baptism is a channel of grace without which none receive it.

The saddest corollary that flowed from this doctrine was that by which Augustine was forced to assert that all those who died unbaptized, including infants, are finally lost and depart into eternal punishment. He did not shrink from the inference, although he assigned the place of lightest punishment in hell to those who were guilty of no sin but original sin, but who had departed this life without having washed this away in the 'laver of regeneration.' This is the dark side of his soteriology; but it should be remembered that it was not his theology of grace, but the universal and traditional belief in the necessity of baptism for remission of sins, which he inherited in common with all of his time, that forced it upon him. The theology of grace was destined in the hands of his successors, who have rejoiced to confess that they were taught by him, to remove this stumbling-block also from Christian teaching; and if not to Augustine, it is to Augustine's theology that the Christian world owes its liberation from so terrible and incredible a tenet. Along with the doctrine of infant damnation, another stumbling-block also, not so much of Augustineian, but of Church theology, has gone. It was not because of his theology of grace, or of his doctrine of predestination, that Augustine taught that comparatively few of the human race are saved. It was, again, because he believed that baptism and incorporation into the visible Church were necessary for salvation. And it is only because of Augustine's theology of grace, which places man in the hands of an all-merciful Saviour and not in the grasp of a human institution, that men can see that in the salvation of all who die in infancy, the invisible Church of God embraces the vast majority of the human race — saved not by the washing of water administered by the Church, but by the blood of Christ administered by God's own hand outside of the ordinary channels of his grace. We are indeed born in sin, and those that die in infancy are, in Adam, children of wrath even as others; but God's hand is not shortened by the limits of His Church on earth, that it cannot save. In Christ Jesus, all souls are the Lord's, and only the soul that itself sinneth shall die (Ezek. xviii. 1-4); and the only judgment wherewith men shall be judged proceeds on the principle that as many as have sinned without law shall also perish without law, and as many as have sinned under law shall be judged by the law (Rev. ii. 12).

Thus, although Augustine's theology had a very strong churchly element within it, it was, on the side that is presented in the controversy against Pelagianism, distinctly anti-ecclesiastical. Its central thought was the absolute dependence of the individual on the grace of God in Jesus Christ. It made everything that concerned salvation to be of God, and traced the source of all good to Him. 'Without me ye can do nothing,' is the inscription on one side of it; on the other stands written, 'All things are yours.' Augustine held that he who builds on a human foundation builds on sand, and founded all his hope on the Rock itself. And there also he founded his teaching; as he distrusted man in the matter of salvation, so he distrusted him in the form of theology. No other of the fathers so conscientiously wrought out his theology from the revealed Word; no other of them so sternly excluded human additions. The subjects of which theology treats, he declares, are such as 'we could by no means find out unless we believed them on the testimony of Holy Scripture.' 'Where Scripture gives no certain testimony,' he says, 'human presumption must beware how it decides in favor of either side.' 'We must first bend our necks to the authority of Scripture,' he insists, 'in order that we may arrive at knowledge and understanding through faith.' And this was not merely his theory, but his practice. No theology was ever, it may be more broadly asserted, more conscientiously wrought out from the Scriptures. Is it without error? No; but its errors are on the surface, not of the essence. It leads to God, and it came from God; and in the midst of the controversies of so many ages it has shown itself an edifice whose solid core is built out of material 'which cannot be shaken.'

www.ingramcontent.com/pod-product-compliance
Lightning Source LLC
Chambersburg PA
CBHW031410040426
42444CB00005B/496